Other books by Ralph T. Ward:

Steamboats: A History of the Early Adventure

Ships through History

PIRATES IN HISTORY

RALPH T. WARD

YORK PRESS BALTIMORE

Library of Congress Cataloging in Publication Data
Ward, Ralph T.
　Pirates in history.

　Bibliography: p.
　1. Pirates. I. Title.
G535.W37　　　　　910'.453　　　　74-14595
ISBN 0-912752-04-1

This book was manufactured in the United States of America.

Library of Congress Catalog Card Number **74-14595**

ISBN 0-912752-04-1

To Marvin Ware Proffitt

CONTENTS

Preface

The story of piracy (and included here are many instances of privateering) parallels the story of maritime development and encompasses some of the most curious episodes in the history of man. Piracy has been a major feature of life at sea since seafarers set sail on the waters of the Persian Gulf from the ports of Sumer, the earliest civilization with a written language. Piracy flourished in all parts of the world until the establishment of steam-powered navies, and at times forced nations to use the severest measures of suppression or face ruin.

The influence of piracy on the course of history, however, has been overlooked, by and large, because historians have so often focused their attention on the campaigns of armies and on the activities on land of kings, parliaments, and congresses. Yet, events at sea from the earliest historical times have had a profound effect on the growth and sustaining power of nations. Piracy is an integral part of that story.

This book has been written to bring together under one cover the most important aspects of the story of piracy and to show the impact of piracy on history.

1. The Earliest Pirates

For thousands of years wherever there have been ships at sea, piracy has been a fact of life. The earliest mention of pirate raids come to us from Sumerian, Babylonian, and Egyptian records. Perhaps the first mention of such raiding is reported in the cuneiform writing developed in the land of Sumer about five thousand years ago. Sumer was a loosely knit group of cities situated between and along the Tigris and Euphrates Rivers in Asia Minor, in the area encompassed by today's Iraq. It stretched from the site of modern Baghdad to the Persian Gulf.

Today, reading the fragile fragments of the clay tablets on which ancient scribes of the Near East wrote, we see numerous references to trade and travel by sea. On such tablets we find an official Sumerian history written over 4,000 years ago that describes the Guti, a barbaric people "who could not be held back." When they descended on Sumer "the riders on the sea could not sail their boats" because they were not safe from attack. These raids on land and at sea caused inflation, famine, misery, and death in the land of Sumer.

A heroic poem of the third millennium B.C. tells of the Sumerians themselves raiding "from the sea to the cedar mountains," that is, using the Tigris and Euphrates Rivers and raiding from the Persian Gulf to the inland mountain ranges. Vessels using the rivers were captured, and sometimes burned. The particular piratical activities mentioned were carried out by a priest. He promised the people of Sumer that he would return safely with boats "heavily laden with

1

spoils." The people believed his boast and invested in the adventure, giving the priest gold, silver, and the necessary supplies. But the priest was a blunderer. He muddled from one serious mistake to the next. Finally he was killed because of his incompetence and his body was thrown into the Euphrates. Had he been successful, most likely he would have been greeted with cheers and honors on his return, as thousands of years later Sir Francis Drake was welcomed home by the mobs of London after his piratical exploit against the Spanish in the New World.

Along with these and other indications of piratical forays, we find the first law against piracy in the history of man. It is written in Babylonian cuneiform script as part of the code of Hammurabi (ca. 1948–1905 B.C.), the sixth king of the first dynasty of Babylonia, who was a capable and wise ruler. He made his city of Babylon supreme throughout the Fertile Crescent, the arc-shaped region from the Levant to the Persian Gulf. The code of law he established was inscribed on an upright monument that can be seen today in Paris in

"Foreign" ship in Egyptian port painted on an ancient decorated pot. It is similar to those found on ancient Tigris-Euphrates Valley cylinder seals. This was the type of craft used by Sumerian raiders.

Babylonia ca. 1900 B.C.

the Louvre. Hammurabi's law code is one of the most impressive ancient documents to survive the centuries.

The inclusion of the law against piracy might seem unusual since Hammurabi's capital, Babylon, was nearly 200 miles from the sea; but there was piracy on the rivers, as well as on the Persian Gulf. Not all of the laws in the code that bears his name were introduced by Hammurabi. The code was a collection of laws from earliest Sumerian times; some had been promulgated by the Sumerian ruler, Lipit-

Ishtar, a descendent of the imperial rulers whose capital had been the city of Ur not far from the Persian Gulf. That the law against piracy was included among the 282 inscribed on the block of black basalt shows that piracy was a continuing and common problem for the ancient Babylonians. The penalty for the seizure of a vessel unlawfully, or by force, was a thirty-fold restitution if the ship belonged to the state or to a religious institution, or a ten-fold restitution if the vessel belonged to a private citizen. If he could not pay the fine, the pirate was put to death.

At the same time that the civilizations of Sumer and Babylonia flourished in the Fertile Crescent area, a different civilization was developing in the eastern Mediterranean on the island of Crete. Bronze Age civilization arose in Crete about 3400 B.C., and Cretan kings ruled the Aegean Sea from about 2000 to 1400 B.C. As Thucydides tells us, "Minos of Crete is the first to whom tradition ascribes a navy." It was Minos who became ruler of the Hellenic world, and "it

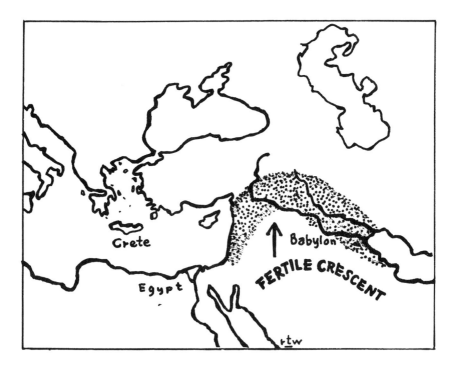

The Fertile Crescent.

was he who, from a natural desire to protect his growing revenues, sought, as far as he was able, to clear the sea of pirates."

Thucydides probably mixed mythology with fact, as ancient historians often did, for the Minos he is speaking of was a mythological figure. There is no reason to doubt, however, that the commercially powerful sea kings of Crete (called Minos always, after the son of Zeus) suppressed piracy by patrolling the seas. Cnossus, the Cretan capital with its fabulous palace and harbor, and other Cretan cities, were not walled. Yet, they were free of raids and free of piracy for centuries, which suggests that pirates had little chance of survival in the well-policed seas around Crete.

Thucydides says that communication by sea became more general after the powerful Minos expelled the pirates. Although the Cretan kings extended their control over neighboring islands and over the mainland in Asia Minor and Europe, the Cretan navy could not always protect the coast of the mainland from pirates. As trade

Ships of Crete, as shown on engraved seals. With such ships Minos, the first sea-king of Crete, cleared the sea of pirates. These ships were also used to patrol the waters around Crete.

flourished the people along the seacoast prospered and began to live in a more settled manner. They grew rich and built walled cities to protect themselves from sea raiders, "for the piratical tribes [of the coast] plundered not only one another, but all those, who, without being seamen, lived on the seacoast." Eventually these bold raiders grew so strong that they conquered and subdued Crete, and devastated Cretan civilization.

Piracy also was common in Egyptian waters for centuries. During the reign of Pepi II (Neferkare), who is supposed to have ruled the Egyptian empire for an incredible ninety-four years over 4,000 years ago, there is a record of Bedouin pirates attacking ships carrying precious cargoes to Egypt via the Red Sea.

The earliest known representation of a seagoing ship which was not a river boat was carved on the wall of a temple built during the reign of Sahure, a king of Egypt in the twenty-eighth century B.C. This ship was part of a fleet that the king sent to raid on the coast of Syria. The raids were successful and the ships returned with prisoners. An earlier king of Egypt, Snofru, sent ships to Byblos in Phoenicia; no drawings of these sea vessels have been discovered. It is believed that Egyptians were sailing the sea as far as to Crete before the year 3000 B.C. The seagoing vessels they used were made from the famous cedars of Lebanon, the stately tree native to Asia Minor, often mentioned in the Bible.

Nile River craft. When pirates attacked such craft, Pharoah Harmhab set exile and mutilation as the punishment for those who were caught.

During the reign of Amenhotep III (1411–1375 B.C.), father of Amenhotep IV (Akhnaton) who is generally known as the first monotheist, Egypt was reaching its greatest glory. But now aggressive enemies began to undermine the power of the ancient empire. They attacked the territories held by the empire outside of Egypt. Coming probably from Lycia in Asia Minor, roving bands of looters infested the eastern Mediterranean, boldly entered the harbors of Cyprus, and raided the Egyptian Delta. Amenhotep III, concerned over the loss of the revenue as a result of the ships' being attacked, created a special squad of marine police, supplementing the ordinary patrol. They constantly guarded the mouth of the river, kept it closed to all but lawful voyagers, and also began collecting a tax from the vessels using the Nile, a profitable sideline for the king, offsetting his losses from pirates.

Amenhotep III had an idea who was causing mischief on the Nile, the lifeline of Egyptian life. He believed the king of Cyprus responsible for instigating the attacks; so he wrote him a letter, still existent, blaming him for sending looters against Egypt, and demanding that the attacks cease. The king of Cyprus denied that he or his people were responsible for any outrage against the mighty Amenhotep. He boldly declared that, "If Cyprians are at sea as pirates I'll punish them." This was merely a diplomatic way of claiming innocence, for no one king or community had the sea-power to deal with the plundering hordes of the time. Only portions of the main sea lanes, rivers and harbors could be patrolled or protected. There were no watches set on small settlements along the coast, or over long stretches between ports. To maintain such watches on land or at sea would have been a gigantic undertaking, an enterprise which would have involved building an enormous permanent navy backed by land forces stationed along the coast. Standing armies and navies are seldom encountered in ancient history. Large forces were raised on a temporary basis; during interims of peace they were disbanded, or due to neglect they decayed.

Egypt had laws against piracy. One such law was issued by Harmhab (reigned about 1350–1315 B.C.) who left many detailed accounts of the wealth and elegance of his time. Part of Harmhab's edict reads, "If the poor man, in order to serve the pharoah, made for himself a craft with its sails. . . . and he was robbed of the craft and the dues, the poor man stood reft of his goods and stripped of his many labors. This is wrong, and the pharoah will suppress it by excellent measures." The "excellent measures," employed to protect the royal revenues arising from goods being carried on vessels on the Nile, were that the thief's "nose shall be cut off, and he exiled to Tharu."

During the thirteenth century B.C., the Egyptians had more to worry about than simple piracy. During the reign of Ramses II, who ruled for sixty-seven years from 1292 to 1225 B.C. and who is commonly thought to be the pharaoh who enslaved the Hebrews, Egypt was faced with a virtual invasion by fleets of pirates. These pirates who raided in Egypt were the settled peoples of Greece, as well as Sardinians, Etruscans, and other tribes being driven out of Asia Minor by a great Indo-European invasion. Barbaric tribes from the East were overrunning Greece and Asia Minor with a fierce and deadly rapidity. They killed, burned, tortured, and plundered. Peaceful herdsmen fled with their families. Some went to Syria, Phoenicia, or Palestine, where they were welcomed and soon intergrated with the established tribes. Others turned to the sea for survival while seeking new homes.

Those who attempted to settle in Egypt were not welcomed. With the barbaric Indo-Europeans at their back, and the powerful Egyptians resisting their attempts to settle, the homeless fugitives were forced to turn to piracy. An Egyptian chronicle tells us that they spent their time "going about the land fighting, to fill their bodies daily." Such fighting was only natural, for they were without land on which to tend flocks or grow grain, and they were hungry. From the sea Egypt looked like a pleasant refuge; but Ramses II did not want the foreigners in Egypt, and under his determined leadership the Egyptians killed, or captured as slaves, thousands of the raiders. Not until shortly after 1200 B.C., however, were these people of the sea finally driven out of Egyptian waters.

The defeat of the sea-people came during the reign of the great warrior king, Ramses III, who left detailed accounts of his brillant campaigns on land and sea against Egypt's enemies. In one of these accounts Ramses III tells how his vessels were protected on long voyages. The ancient inscription reads that the king made "transports, galleys, and barges upon the sea, with archers equipped with

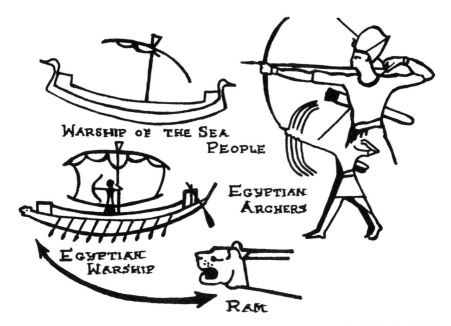

Illustrations from a relief in a temple near Thebes in Egypt describing the defeat (ca. 1200 B.C.) of the sea people. This relief is the first picture in history of a sea battle.

arms, in order to safely transport products from countries at the ends of the earth." Both during the earlier periods and later, water patrols protected ships along the sea lanes by stationing soldiers aboard ship, and cruising police up and down the Nile. The river force was similar to the present-day coast guard.

In a temple near Thebes a relief with an inscription tells of the defeat of the sea peoples. The relief is the first picture of naval action in history, and is quite vivid. The description of the battle is rather bombastic, and exceedingly boastful, as were all such wordy tributes to ancient Egyptian rulers. It states that "the northern countries, which are in their isles, are restless in their limbs; they infect the sea routes of the harbor mouths." We can easily imagine fleets of the fugitives loitering near Egyptian harbors, where the scavenging would be most profitable. The account goes on to tell of the cities these wandering peoples attacked, and how they desolated the pharoah's helpless people and "laid their hands upon the land." This last deed was unforgiveable in the pharoah's eyes because he, and he alone, could deal with matters pertaining to the land which Egypt held. So, he gathered his war council and had soldiers and ships "prepared and armed to trap them like wild fowl."

His enemies were good fighters, especially the fierce and dangerous Sardinians; but they had been overwhelmed at home and now, living at sea, they were at a disadvantage. Using galleys packed with archers and other warriors, the Egyptians slaughtered the enemy until the dead made "heaps from stern to bow" in their ships. Ramses III, acting like a "goring bull," gave them such a stunning setback that they left Egyptian waters and dispersed.

The results of this great sea battle were that the Sardinians sailed to the island that still bears their name; the Etruscans went to the west coast of Italy; and it is likely that the sea people the Egyptians called the *Sikels* took possession of the island of Sicily at this time. The date of their arrival in Sicily, given by the Greek historians Hellanikos and Thucydides, is 1150 B.C., which seems close enough to their defeat in Egypt to agree historically.

During their many years of wandering, the sea people had gone from piracy to an allied effort at war. Although they were defeated, this pattern has been repeated so often in history that piracy appears as an omnious first step to migration and conquest. In this instance, the settlement of these groups in the western Miditerranean brought the first civilized peoples from the Near East to that section. They had great influence on the future development of Europe, especially the gifted Etruscans who considerably affected the culture of Rome.

2. Pirates of the Phoenician World

The Phoenicians have often been called the "dreadful pirates" of ancient times. They were Canaanites who inhabited a strip of land bordering the eastern Mediterranean in Asia Minor. As a people they were never a strong nor a well-organized nation, but rather a group of wealthy cities such as Tyre, Sidon, and Byblos, located in present-day Lebanon. They were probably the first to use the double-tiered warship, and in their sturdy "round" (i.e., broad) merchant vessels they carried the goods of more civilized sections to primitive areas. (Throughout history cargo vessels have tended to be wide, and naval vessels to be long and narrow.) Their manufactured wares, as well as the alphabet that they began to use about 1500 B.C., were welcomed by the less civilized peoples of Europe, especially the Greeks. The Phoenicians took the place of the eclipsed Cretans as the maritime leaders of the Mediterranean. They were the middlemen of the ancient world, and while the Greeks were evolving from primitive tribesmen to competent traders the Phoenicians filled a place in the economic scheme of the Near East that others were not capable of occupying.

Few inscriptions left by the Phoenicians themselves still exist; their story is told mostly by others, the Egyptians, Assyrians, Greeks, and the Hebrews. In the Bible, in the book of the Prophet Ezekiel, we find the Lamentation for Tyre, perhaps the Phoenicians' wealthiest and strongest city. Ezekiel describes the materials used by the Phoenician shipbuilders. The ship boards were made of fir trees from

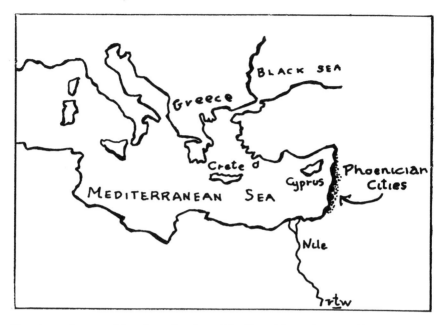

Map shows the general location of such wealthy Phoenician cities as Byblos, Sidon, and Tyre.

Senir; the masts, of cedars from Lebanon; the oars, of oaks from Bashan; benches for the rowers were of ivory; and fine linen from Egypt was used to make the sails. Of course this is an idealized account given to stress the wealth of Tyre, but it supports numerous Greek observations that Phoenicians built the best and sturdiest ships in the world. Ezekiel also mentions some of the crew members aboard these ships. One of the most important was the pilot who charted the day's course (usually from memory), and directed the steersmen at the steeroar. Also mentioned are the caulkers, the men who forced oakum (untwisted pieces of old ropes), or other materials between the ship's planks and boards. This was a crucial task; travelers often complained in ancient times that vessels leaked profusely, and this made ships uncomfortable and unsafe.

The luxury items that the Phoenician ships carried were supplemented by cargoes of slaves. Eumaeus, a herdsman in the Homeric epics, was one of these slaves brought to Greece by the Phoenician merchants. Eumaeus' father, a minor king in a land beyond Sicily, had bought from pirates a slave, a girl from the Phoenician city of

Sidon. The king employed her as a nurse for his son. One day she led the child onto a Phoenician vessel trading in the area, and into slavery. She was now free, but on the voyage home, she tripped and fell into the ship's hold, died, and was thrown overboard. The child was sold in Greece to Odysseus's father.

Herodotus, the Greek historian who wrote the first great prose work in European literature, his monumental *Histories*, mentions that the Phoenicians began making long trading voyages as soon as they settled in their coastal cities, and that they loaded their ships with goods from Egypt and Assyria. He opens the *Histories* recounting an incident when Phoenician traders called at Argos, sold all their wares, and then seized and carried off a number of Greek women. This, Herodotus says, was the initial incident in the conflict between the Greeks and the Asiatic peoples that eventually culminated in the gruesome Persian wars.

Herodotus and other Greek writers often dwell on the subject of kidnapping when talking about the Phoenicians. This, however, appears to be a device to create prejudice against rival traders rather than the unbiased truth, for the main source of slaves sold by the Phoenicians was not Greece, but Africa.

Phoenician explorations were famous in the ancient world. Their circumnavigation of the African continent is still considered an amazing feat. They also ventured out into the Atlantic, knew of the Canary Islands, and perhaps discovered Madeira. They undertook trading missions to the West Coast of Africa. Here they bartered glass items, pottery, metal work, and other articles for gold, ivory, and wild beasts. They also brought back slaves from the Sahara region, an area that was not then a desert to the degree it is today. These slaves were white, of the Libyan people.

Another telling point that does not support the general impression created by those Greeks who pictured the Phoenicians as "horrifying" pirates is that, although their vessels, especially their war galleys, were the models for the nations of the world at the time, their "round" bulky cargo ships were built to safely carry as much merchandise as possible. Pirate ships were usually without much cargo space, which made them light, fast on the attack, and easy to maneuver. Pirate craft usually were either relatively small rowed vessels, or swift sailing ships that could quickly be converted into oared

Phoenician cargo vessel.

vessels during an attack. Some groups of pirates used craft as small as life-boats, some even used rafts. The bulky Phoenician cargo vessels were certainly not used primarily for piracy.

Although the famous Phoenician warships and transports were hired by foreign governments, the early Phoenicians of the eastern Mediterranean had neither navy nor army of their own. On their trading voyages they sailed in heavily laden ships, as they did on returning to their coastal cities. Frequently trading voyages took years, sometimes two or three, sometimes longer. Their heavy ships, the volume of their trade, and the fact that the Greeks as well as others warmly welcomed such trading missions, all seem to indicate that the Phoenicians were generally peaceful merchants and not looters. That they did act as kidnappers along the coast at times means only that they behaved in a manner common to the period.

3. The Noble Pirates of Greece

The sea-coast dwellers of the Greek peninsula mentioned by Thucydides who "plundered not only one another, but all those who, without being seamen, lived on the seacoast," were Achaeans, a tribe of Indo-Europeans who probably migrated to the Greek peninsula from the region of the Caspian Sea. Eventually they settled in Greece at Tiryns and Mycenae, cities that had been highly developed under the control of the Cretan sea kings. Once settled, the Achaeans built strongholds. These migrants were rude herdsmen and savage fighters, but contact with the prosperous maritime civilization of Crete tamed them somewhat. Settled life introduced them to the art of sailing—and the business of piracy.

When the Mycenaean script was deciphered a short time ago, historians discovered to their surprise that the people of Mycenae and Tiryns on the mainland had thrown off Cretan dominance about 1400 B.C., invaded the island, and devasted the Cretan world. During the following centuries the Achaeans, or Mycenaeans, were in control of the Aegean. They were not peaceful traders as the Cretans had been, nor, evidently, good neighbors. They were addicted to raiding, piracy and war. With the restraints imposed by Cretan sea power removed, the Mycenaean nobles did not develop trade with its steady profits; instead they pursued the irregular but quicker profits of piracy.

During the period that the Mycenaean civilization thrived, pillaging raids were common as far as Egypt, a five-day sail from Crete.

Map shows general location of Mycenae and Tiryns whose inhabitants were addicted to war and piracy.

Their raids and wars in Asia Minor are well known. The destruction of Troy was one of their last acts. The Mycenaeans' terrifying behavior made such an impression on the area that tales of their adventures became the subject of many later Greek poems that are still read today, especially the Homeric epics. In such tales "sacker of cities," and "raider," are used as titles of honor; the more brutal and destructive a warrior, the more he was praised by his fellow Mycenaeans. The successful raider supplied his community with glory as well as booty such as cattle and slaves.

The prevalence of piracy in the epics might seem to indicate that at the time any man in Greece could, if he wanted, undertake a piractical raid. But piracy, in fact, had a curiously restricted pattern. Thucydides tells us that ". . .old poets represent people everywhere

Above: Greek nobles sailing as pirates. Both vessels have fighting decks; rowers can be seen below the warriors. *Below*: An enlargement of the rowers, showing a Greek vessel of about 700 B.C. This vase painting, signed "Aristonothos," is one of the earliest signed works of art in Europe. Much of the paint has flaked off, but the vessel can be seen to be a galley.

asking of voyagers, 'Are you pirates.' as if those who were asked would have no inclination to disclaim the suggestion. . . ." The works of the old poets Thucydides speaks of—Homer, Hesiod, and others— show that his statement is a simplification. It must be understood that raiders were not so politely greeted anywhere unless they were members of the noble class on a peaceful visit.

In Book III of the Odyssey, Lord Nestor asks his guest Telémakhos, the noble son of Odysseus, who comes ashore on a visit with his friends, "Who are you strangers, and by what sea route did you get here? Are you on a trading voyage, or do you risk your chances at sea as pirates, for at hazard of their own lives they wander, bringing harm to other men." Again in Book IX we find the exact words Lord Nestor used repeated, but this time the question is asked of Odysseus in the land of Cyclops. These are the words that Thucydides is probably referring to, but they imply no casual acceptance of pirates or piracy. They simply state the facts of life at the time: piracy was common, and it brought harm to some, rewards to others.

The rewards went to the warrior nobles who went on raiding expeditions as a matter of course. They also went on trading expeditions. If the results of trading were not up to expectations, they might raid and plunder to make up for the expense of the voyage. Farmers and makers of pottery went to sea also, as did workers in metal who carried their anvils and tools with them. These people went to sea to sell their goods and services, not as pirates. Although Homer does not tell us about the lives of such men, Hesiod does, especially in his *Works and Days.*

People did not leisurely inquire of strangers appearing on their shores if they were pirates. They did quite the opposite—they fled in terror, sometimes merely at the sight of a strange ship. Slave raids were so common that sea-coast or island people did not take chances with unknown voyagers. In isolated coastal areas, the sound of dogs barking at night was taken as a warning for the inhabitants to hide their valuables and flee.

Fear of Mycenean or other pirates often forced the people of small coastal villages to join together to build fortified settlements for protection, or to move inland, away from the sea. A fortified settlement might simply be a walled encampment, or it might include a tower with a courtyard. The tower held the people during an attack, the courtyard was used for the livestock.

Eventually the Hellenic Dorians conquered and replaced the Mycenaeans in Greece. The Dorian invasion, which was in full swing after 1200 B.C., was so relentless and widespread, that it forced a shift in population. Many Myceneans fled, as did the peaceful Ionians who left Peloponnesus for the Aegean islands and Asia Minor. The Hellenic Dorians, or Greeks, had a number of attitudes that were similar to those of their predecessors, especially their pastorally oriented thinking. The ideal life, according to the noblest of Greeks, was fashioned after the rural existence of their gods and goddesses. To the early Hellenic Dorians, trade although not exactly shameful was not the most honorable occupation, and it was left to foreigners, the *metics* who were resident aliens. Raiding and piracy, however, carried no mark of disgrace; fighting, like being a herdsman, was considered manful and respectable. Over the centuries this attitude was greatly modified. The Hellenic Dorians, or Greeks, merged with other tribes on the Greek peninsula and in Asia Minor. Eventually

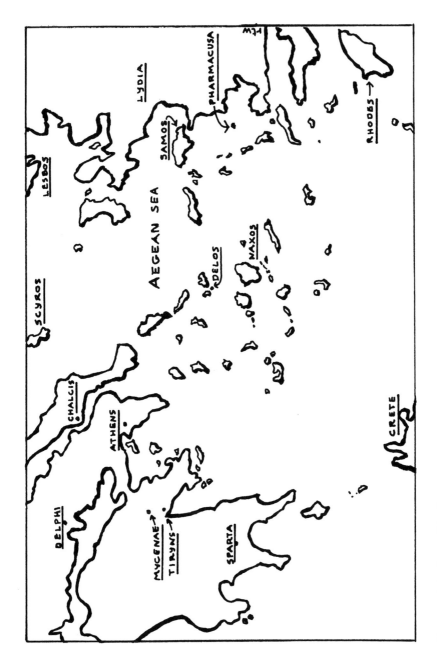

Greece and the Aegean Islands.

they took to the sea, carried on peaceful trade and became a commercially powerful people who colonized large areas of the Mediterranean.

Piracy seems to have been prevalent throughout Greek history. Much of the piracy in ancient Greece, however, was actually privateering, that is, piracy conducted by an individual operating with government approval against hostile forces. Usually these private men-of-war sought to capture merchant ships. In ancient Greece "hostile force" or "enemy" might mean anyone from a commercial rival to an actual warring enemy.

Throughout Greek history there was a fierce desire for local independence combined with a warriors' aim to dominate nearby settlements. More often than not this made Greek unity impossible. There was no strong central government to curb lawlessness at sea over the vast area controlled by various Greek tribes; therefore during most of ancient Greek history piracy was part of the violent and competitive life in Greek settlements and cities.

In the good sailing months of summer—Hesiod tells us that the season for navigation lasted only fifty days—many fighting men took to the sea to raid their neighbor's shipping. Such actions often were fully backed by local governments, so what appears to be piracy was privateering in many cases. The difference is important, for although their methods may overlap, the aims of pirates and privateers are poles apart. The privateer strives to make his government strong by weakening an enemy at sea. He may grow rich in the process, but if he is successful, the result is beneficial to his city or state. The pirate operates against all cities and states; he brings "harm" to all men indiscriminately.

When the noble Solon, who was a descendant of the ancient kings of Athens, was elected the chief officer of that city in 594 B.C., a law was enacted that stressed the enforceability of private contracts between "pirates or merchants" unless the contracts contravened public enactments. This did not, most probably, mean all pirates, but only Athenian pirates, and possibly only those operating in other waters, or against foreigners.

Naturally the Athenians took a dim view of piracy when it was directed against them. In the middle of the 460s B.C., when Athens was a leader in the Hellenic world, the island of Scyros (situated between the Greek peninsula and the Hellespont), which had for a long time been the center of piracy, was attacked by the Athenian fleet under Cimon, the son of a hero in the Persian wars. The pirates of Scyros were captured and sold into slavery. This action was taken to protect the main Athenian shipping route from the Black Sea. Once it was cleared of sea-raiders, the island was settled by Athenians, securing it against the return of pirates to the area. Yet, rival shipping that passed the island was subject to the attack at sea from the newly settled Athenians. This was "piracy" to the ships attacked, but "privateering" to the Athenians.

An inscription from the Greek island of Samos (just off the coast of present-day Turkey, and still Greek) states clearly that in the 500s B.C. plundering at sea was carried on with the approval of the goddess Hera, as well as with the consent of the state.

Polycrates, the tyrant of Samos, ruled at this time. He was a great sailor and shipowner who used his ships in naval and piratical operations, as well as for peaceful trade. His seizures were on a grand scale, for he stopped all shipping that passed, in effect forming a blockade. Polycrates took possession of craft operated by what he considered hostile seamen, that is either foreigners or fellow Greeks who were against his rule. He is supposed jokingly to have explained that in this way he harmed his enemies whose ships he kept, and gained the gratitude of his friends whose ships he released. It was, however, no joke; it was the serious business of privateering. The ships captured were rich prizes, they and their cargoes, when sold, put a great deal of gold and silver into Polycrates' treasury. The loss of such vessels weakened rivals, and strengthened the tyrannical hold Polycrates had on the island of Samos.

How complicated the business of piracy and privateering was in ancient Greece is shown by the text of a treaty between two small cities on the Corinthian Gulf. (Corinth and other cities on the Gulf were commercially important as early as the eighth century B.C.) The treaty, inscribed on a bronze tablet of the 400s B.C., and now in the British Museum, reads:

No man of Oiantheia, if he makes a seizure, shall carry off a Chaleian merchant from Chaleian soil, nor a Chaleian an Oiantheian merchant from Oiantheian soil. Nor shall either seize a merchant's cargo within the territory of the other city. If any one breaks this rule, he may lawfully be seized on the sea without incurring the penalty, except in the actual harbor of the city.

If piracy was so common, why did the Greeks travel so often by sea? If you had asked a Greek loitering in the market place of ancient Athens this question, he would most likely have thought you were quite mad, for the reasons were so obvious to him. "We travel by sea," he might say, "because it's so easy and so safe." Even with the threat of pirates, travel on the sea was easier and safer than on land. The much-indentured coastline and the many obstructing mountains on the Greek peninsula made land travel difficult, with the roads rough, gutted, and poorly cared-for. In addition, when a traveler voyaged on the sea he was not forced to pass through barbarian territory or face the hoards of bandits ever present in the hills and on the roads. Travel by land was not only more dangerous than by sea, it was also more costly and often slower.

Greek seamen, like the earlier seamen of Egypt and other civilizations, were restricted to well-known and well-traveled sea lanes. Merchants were called "cross-channel men" because they went from bay to bay, and island to island. Vessels, as they had from earliest times, almost always stayed close to land, and this was, of course, one of the reasons piracy was so common; the ships were easily assaulted. In the less developed parts of Greece it was considered an honest occupation to hold up or cut out a merchant ship bound for other areas. How else could people in such poor and backward settlements get luxuries from wealthier areas? They had little to barter; there was little inducement for merchants to stop in the area. If the gods did not intend the ships to be pirated, why did they force them to hug the shore so invitingly close?

Educated Greek navigators relied on a course set out by a guide called a "periplus." Such an itinerary described coastal landmarks, safe harbors, and water supplies. It might say "the coast here is rocky, irregular, and destitute of safe beaches. It must always be avoided." These itineraries were available to the educated seamen, but the world at sea was primarily peopled by uneducated men from small maritime communities where the inhabitants depended on tradition and oral guidance. (As late as the 1590s, Francesco Carletti, a traveling merchant of Florence, wrote that most pilots ordinarily did not know how to read.) The unsophisticated seaman, if he went into unkown waters, was not aware of the places where pirates operated, so he was especially subject to attack.

Even knowledgeable long-distance traders were continually exposed and assailable. There were few voyages made on the open sea, and even these ended with coastwise travel. The exceptionally long voyage from Crete to Egypt took five days and five nights; in ancient times it was a really bold adventure, undertaken only in the summer when the etesian winds blew steadily toward the south and carried a vessel to the African or Near Eastern coast. Once arrived, however, the trader stayed a long time selling, trading, and buying goods to carry back on the return voyage. The journey back was not made directly from Egypt to Crete, for the wind blew to the north only during the winter months, a time when vessels were put into winter sheds for repair and storage. A captain left Egypt in the spring, followed the shore along the coast of Asia Minor, and then might trade at Cyprus before arriving back at Crete.

The Greeks knew much about the movement of the stars, but they did not often use their knowledge at sea. They did not usually sail at night, though to do so would have helped them in evading pirates. Day or night, out of sight of land and without a compass, the ancient Greeks would have been hopelessly lost in the unmarked world of the open sea.

Voyages were exceedingly dangerous, so ships often traveled in groups. Travel by fleet for reasons of safety was the rule in long-distance trade, especially if the ships were fairly large and the cargo reasonably valuable. (This was true through the Middle Ages, and up until recent times.) It did not hold for smaller vessels, however, for their cargoes were seldom worth the trouble involved in arranging fleet movement. Such vessels went on "free" voyages, often as "tramps," stopping wherever cargo was available. "Tramp" is not a derogatory term, it merely means to go in steps; its counterpart would be a vessel that runs regularly between ports, often on a fixed schedule.

The sort of ships favored by Greek pirates were small, swift ones. The type of vessel Odysseus is so often pictured as using, called a *myoparone*, was a fighting ship with both oars and sail. There was

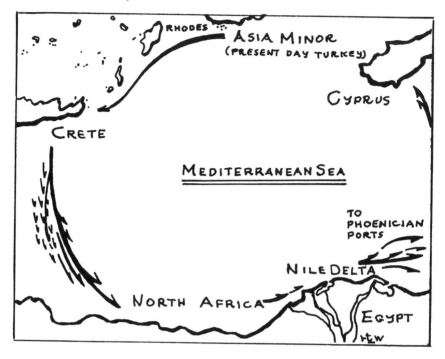

Ancient sailing routes between Crete and Africa.

also the *camaras*, especially favored by pirates of the Black Sea. This was a light flat-bottomed, low boat capable of holding 25 to 30 men. The *camaras* were double-ended craft; like canoes, they had both ends constructed so they could easily be drawn ashore. The oars on this vessel were arranged for rowing either way, useful for easy maneuverability. Sea raiders who operated from the coast used fishing boats, or even small row-boats, and they went out in flotillas to attack passing ships. These boats were sometimes so small that they could be hauled on a wagon. (The *camara* could also be lifted into or out of the water; it could be taken from a hiding place and quickly launched, to the surprise of a passing vessel.) Theophrastus, an Athenian scholar of the late 300s B.C., said that the typical raiding boat of his day was the *hemiolia*. This was either a one-and-a-half or a two-tiered ship, that is a ship with two levels of oarsmen to a side. Then there were what the Greeks called "race horses," small dispatch boats, usually built during war, but also used successfully for piracy.

Vessels showing the adventures of Odysseus. *a,* painted in 200–100 B.C.; *b,* painted in 500–450 B.C. The circle at the bow represents an eye. Such eyes were provided so the ship could "see" where it was going. There seemed nothing odd about this, since when vessels put to sea in the spring they were blessed (as they still are with a bottle of champagne) and put under the protection of a god or goddess. (Even today in Greek maritime communities the blessing of vessels in spring is common.) The eyes, therefore, represented the eyes of the god. The eye of god remains a popular theme in Mediterranean cultures, and eyes are still sometimes painted on the bows of small vessels in the Mediterranean.

Greek ships were painted many different colors, the paint being applied with melted wax to help protect the wood. Red or black were favored, but purple, blue, white, yellow, orange, and green were also used. There was another color that was said to match the color of the waves; it was applied to ships used in reconnoitering during war. This wave-colored paint, perhaps a blue-grey or some such inconspicuous natural fog- or sea-like hue, was sometimes used by pirates. It enabled their vessels to blend with the surroundings as they waited in ambush in a cove or inlet.

It is easy to imagine such camouflaged vessels concealed in the narrow creek-like inlet on which the settlement of Trotilon (modern La Bruca) grew in Sicily. The growth of such colonies was often

89231

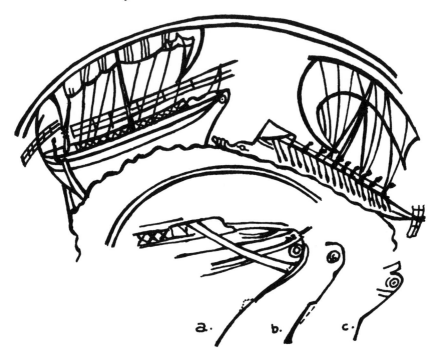

A Greek merchant vessel, 550–450 B.C. (*left*), and a war galley (*right*). These are often interpreted as being a merchantman and a pirate ship, although they could just as well represent a merchant vessel being convoyed by a warship. *a.* a detail of the bow. *b.* the dotted line shows a part of the bow that is often omitted in modern drawings of this vessel. *c.* this omission leads to the bow's being described incorrectly as similar to the bow of a clipper ship, as shown in this drawing.

accompanied by piracy by the colonists. One author, Ephorus, wrote that before the earliest Greek colonies were found in Sicily "men were so afraid of the pirate vessels of the Tyrrhenians (Etruscans) and the savagery of the barbarians (Sikels) in this region that they would not sail there for trading." This was the situation the colonizing Greeks faced; thus Zancle (present-day Messina) and other Greek colonies in Sicily were founded by warriors who plundered and raided in the region. When such outposts became strong enough, peaceful pioneering Greeks followed, built, and settled.

It did not always go well with Greeks settling in foreign parts. When they tried to take over certain regions in the western Mediterranean the Carthaginians and Etruscans, the leading non-Greek powers of the area, joined forces to drive them out. The naval battle that these combined forces fought against the Greek pirates off

Alalia (on Corsica) in the year 540 B.C., in which Greeks from Asia Minor were defeated, is regarded as the incident which contained the colonizing efforts of the Greeks in the west.

In the Black Sea settlements that the Greeks prized so highly, the story was somewhat different. When the Greeks began to infiltrate and colonize in the 600s B.C., trading wine, oil, and other Greek products for the minerals of the region, some of the natives of the place began growing grain for export to Greek cities. Many of the coastal tribes in the area, however, took to piracy. In their swift *camaras* they would swoop down on the now peacefully trading Greeks.

During the fifth century B.C. trade came fully into its own in ancient Greece. The Greeks had developed the alphabet (adopted from the Phoenicians), and this made communication easier among distant people, and promoted long-distance trade. The Greeks also had coinage for a workable exchange in place of barter. Over the centuries they had acquired a respect for professional seamen and

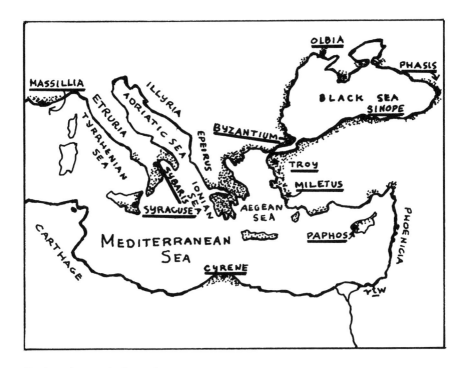

Greek settlements in the Mediterranean.

traders. While during the early periods of ancient Greek history piracy was the general condition at sea amongst the noble warriers class, with the development of trade and the necessity of importing goods other than mere novelties, piracy was often suppressed, directed, or restricted by the later Greek city-states.

The Greeks had taken a long journey from their barbaric beginnings. It would be wrong, however, to think that piracy was stamped out. Demosthenes, the Athenian demagogue and orator, tells of a man who, going off to search for a runaway slave, was captured by pirates, chained, and sold. A friend came to the captive's aid and pledged his goods and property to help raise money for his release. (Demosthenes' moral was: life is filled with perils, and when trouble strikes the best security was not the state, but friendship. Indirectly, Demosthenes also showed that pirates still supplied the slave market, and life was not so idyllic in ancient Greece as the poets sometimes make it seem.)

4. Rome Rules

Three Delphic envoys returning from Rome in 188–189 B. C. were murdered near the island of Cephalonia (Kefalliñia) at the mouth of the Corinthian Gulf. In contemporary documents their deaths were attributed to pirates. Many similar examples late in the Hellenic period (323 to 31 B.C.) indicate that piracy became more frequent as the power of the great Greek cities diminished and the Mediterranean became a Roman sea. Eventually murder, pillage, and the burning of settlements and cities increased to such an extent that the Roman senate was forced to declare a full scale war on piracy.

This surge of piratical activity developed because Rome, at this time, was not interested in policing the Mediterranean. With an inland population of hardworking farmers, there was little concern for maritime activity during the initial period of Rome's growth. Although fierce fighters on land, the Romans left maritime matters in the hands of the Carthaginians, Etruscans, and others. Only after the strong foundations of Rome had been laid did the Romans adapt themselves to the sea, and then only slowly.

Evidence of piracy on the Italian peninsula can be seen on a stele decorated with a relief showing pirates raiding from the sea in an early iron age community. The initial settlements of the Etruscans were often visited by raiders from the most distant points in the western Mediterrean. Because of this many of their settlements were placed inland, although the Etruscans were a seafaring people.

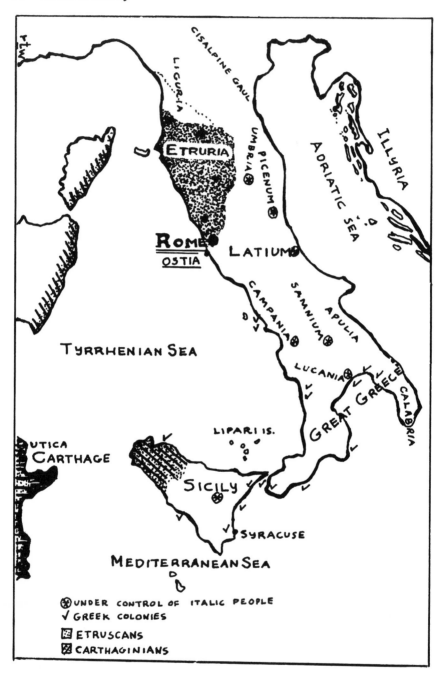

The Italic peninsula before the supremacy of Rome.

Etruscan vessel, 2nd century B.C.

The Etruscans, who had settled north of the Tiber on the western coast of Italy, controlled the arm of the Mediterranean called the Tyrrhenian Sea. When the first Greek settlements were founded in Italy and Sicily, the commercial princes of the Etruscans continued to control the Tyrrhenian Sea by maintaining a naval force composed of pirates. Piracy was part of the Etruscans' trade policy, and it helped them acquire great wealth. Their sea-power was broken by the Greeks when Syracuse, on Sicily, became a strong colony and met and defeated the fleets of Etruscan pirates who had raided boldly in this area for centuries.

The Carthaginians, who were the descendants of Phoenicians who had settled in the western Mediterranean sometime after 1000 B.C., also favored sea-born commerce. They had an excellent reputation so far as maritime affairs were concerned, except for one extremely unpleasant habit—their war galleys usually sank on sight any foreign vessel they encountered. Carthage did not brook commercial rivals. Unlike the Phoenician cities of the East, the Carthaginians had a strong and active navy of their own to protect their shipping and their cities. This was unusual in the ancient world.

Cathage eventually forced Rome to take to the sea. How this came about is an interesting story which began in Sicily in 264 B.C., and led to the eventual downfall of Carthage and the rise of Rome.

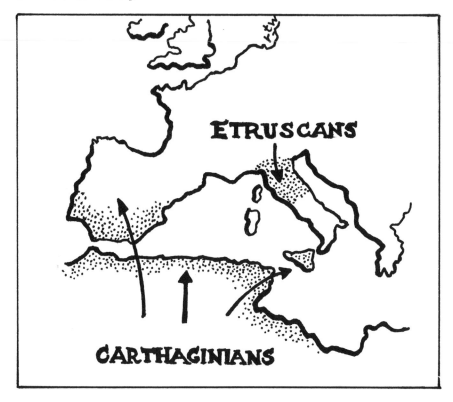

Areas under Carthaginian and Etruscan control.

In 264 B.C. a group of mercenaries for King Hiero of Syracuse left his service, turned pirate, and captured the important Greek colonial city of Zancle (present-day Messina) on Sicily. At the time, Zancle controlled the narrow strait of water that separates Sicily from the Italian mainland. Its inhabitants attacked shipping headed for the north and Rome, and that passing from the north toward eastern parts of the Mediterranean. Once in secure control of Zancle, the pirates raided Roman shipping. They also attacked the shipping of their former employer, King Hiero of Syracuse. Hiero was outraged and tried to suppress them. When he did not succeed, he turned for help to Carthage which dominated a good part of Sicily.

The Carthaginians, anxious to crush piracy in the area, agreed to fight the pirates of Zancle. They landed a garrison at Zancle and began a systematic attack against the pirate stronghold. The pirates in turn appealed to Rome for help. Rome, anxious to gain a foothold in Sicily, and to control of the Strait of Messina, rushed in to battle the Carthaginians. With his army the Roman consul Appius Claudius crossed from Italy to Sicily. It was the first time that a Roman army had left the Italian peninsula, and it was the beginning of the famous and savage Punic Wars, given that name because Punic was the language of the Carthaginians. In Rome the word came to mean painful, treacherous, or perfidious.

Only after many years of fighting, and the building and subsequent loss of many Roman fleets, did Rome finally win the prolonged wars. (There were three main wars: 264–241, 218–201, and 149–146 B.C. It was in the second war that the bold Carthaginian, Hannibal, crossed the Alps.) In 241 B.C. Carthage was forced to cede most of Sicily to Rome. Still the war went on. It did not end until Rome was in complete command of the sea and the city of Carthage utterly destroyed. After the absolute defeat of Carthage, piracy in the area did not decrease—it increased. With the commercial cities of the Etruscans weakened, the Carthaginian navy destroyed, and

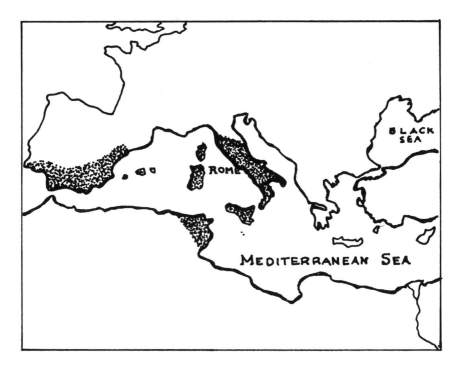

Rome at the end of the Punic Wars.

Rome unwilling to maintain a fleet, there was no effective patrolling force operating in the western Mediterranean. Fleets of pirate vessels roamed at will and went unchallenged.

In the eastern Mediterranean piracy also increased, especially amongst the Illyrians who had their strongholds along the coast of what is present-day Yugoslavia. With light and speedy galleys the Illyrians attacked merchantmen at will in the Adriatic where their control was undisputed. So long as they preyed only on other nations Rome paid scant attention to the Illyrian pirates, but during the last half of the third century B.C. the Illyrians began to venture into other branches of the Mediterranean besides the Adriatic. When they started to attack ships headed for Rome and to rob, capture and kill Roman traders, the Roman senate decided that something must be done to stop the Illyrian pirates.

In 230 B.C. the Roman leaders sent two envoys to the Illyrian court to demand reparations for piratical acts against Romans. The Illyrian queen, Teuta, claimed that her people were not responsible for any outrage, and would not pay. The envoys, the brothers Gaius and Lucius Coruncanius, threatened the queen with retalitory acts, and this so angered Queen Teuta that she broke off negotiations. On their way back to Rome the envoys were attacked by pirates; one of the brothers was killed while the other made his escape. Queen Teuta may or may not have been the instigator of the attack, but she further infuriated Roman sensibilities by flatly refusing to offer any explanation of the incident.

Because of the queen's evident contempt, and the increasingly bold acts of piracy by the Illyrians, the Romans (already introduced to war at sea by the Carthaginians) gathered a great fleet of 200 vessels. In addition to the seamen aboard these ships there were 22,000 hardy Roman soldiers who fought the Illyrians at sea and on land. The success of the soldiers on land, where they attacked and subdued many Illyrian fortresses, brought the pirates to terms. Queen Teuta was compelled to bow before the might of Rome; she was forced to sign a demeaning treaty in which she promised payment of tribute, the abandonment of piracy by her people, and the release of all Greek cities under Illyrian control. The last signaled the beginning of serious Roman influence in Greece which eventually led to Roman conquest in the area.

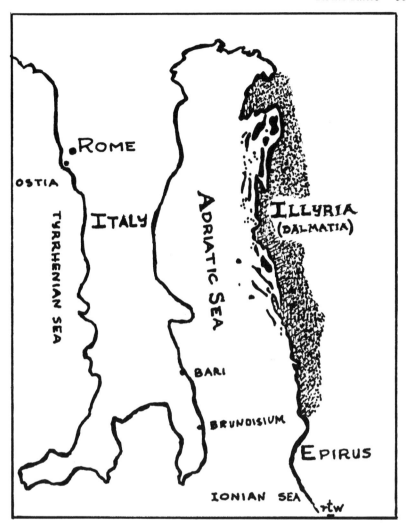

Illyria. The Dalmatian coast has been a stronghold of pirates throughout much of history.

Queen Teuta, who held the Illyrian throne as guardian of her son, was an interesting woman. She was evidently something of an Amazon, for she personally accompanied her Illyrian warriors on their raids, and directed them. Her methods of operation at sea were typical pirate methods. In one typical instance, she and her raiders landed at the city of Epidamnos in the years before her troubles with Rome. Her Illyrians came ashore carrying water jars and cried to the Epidamnosians that they were dying of thirst and desperately in need of water, a plea that no civilized person could decently ignore. Within the water jars, however, the Illyrians had concealed short swords, and once they reached the city gate which opened to them, they killed the guards and began a general attack. The Epidamnosians, although surprised, fought bravely and eventually drove the Illyrians off. Such methods of attack through deceit were used by pirates through the ages on the sea and on land.

A good part of the Illyrian pirate's success before Roman interference can be attributed to the type of ship they used—the Lembi (an Illyrian tribe) galley. This was a two-banked vessel. In such irregular warfare it proved so useful that the Romans eventually modeled one of their own two-banked fighting ships along similar lines. The Roman biremes were called *liburnians*. After about 50 B.C. the name *liburna* was applied indiscriminately to any two-banked vessel in the Roman fleet. Herodotus in the *Histories* mentions that the Illyrian galleys were based on the fifty-man galley of the Phocaeans, Greeks who lived on the Gulf of Corinth.

In their suppression of the Illyrian pirates, and in their war against Carthage, the Romans had taken to the sea to great advantage; but Roman strategists were still not convinced that it was Rome's duty to police the seas. The city of Rome was far enough inland to be reasonably safe from attack from the sea, but near enough, with the use of the port of Ostia at the mouth of the Tiber River, to welcome the many traders who plied the Mediterranean. The Romans thought it especially unnecessary to patrol the eastern

A libruna (from a detail on Trajan's column, 113 A.D.). This type of vessel was originally Illyrian. It proved so effective that the Romans modeled one of their most successful fighting ships along similar lines.

part of the Mediterranean, for it was already policed by the Rhodian navy; Rhodes had taken over that task after the power of Egypt waned.

Efficient Rhodian patrols cruised among the islands of Greece in the Aegean and the Sea of Crete, where they protected not only their own shipping, but all shipping at sea, for much of the cargo on the vessels in these waters was destined for Rhodes. Service in the highly organized naval force was a proud duty of Rhodian citizens. One surviving inscription tells of the death of three sons in one family of Rhodes, two of the men dying in action against Etruscan pirates, and one against other pirates who were not named. There was little protection in the eastern arms of the Mediterranean other than that provided by Rhodes.

During 167–166 B.C., Rome was strong enough to break the naval power of Rhodes when the Rhodians annoyed and angered Rome as Rhodes attempt to intercede during the Third Macedonian War, when Rome and Macedonia were battling for control of the Greek states. Rome, in a fit of spiteful fury, destroyed Rhodes economically by seizing all Rhodian possessions on the mainland of Asia Minor and declaring the small island of Delos, one of the islands of the Cyclades, a free port under the control of Athens. Thereafter, instead of going to Rhodes, traders with their slaves, wines, and other merchandise went to Delos where they could enter free, and trade at the market under the protection of both Rome and Athens. But with the Rhodian navy gone and no Athenian or Roman police force to take its place, pirate fleets virtually took command of the seas in the area.

The pirates grew strong and their fleets eventually acquired secure bases along the rock-bound coast of Cilicia. Located on the mainland of Asia Minor across from Cyprus, Cilicia had always been a pirate stronghold. In the eighth century B.C. the king of Assyria, using Phoenician-built war vessels, caught looters "like fish" along that coast. The difficulty of permanently clearing this particular region of pirates stemmed from the fact that whenever they lost control of the coast the pirates simply scurried inland. Here they could not be pursued because the fiercely independent local tribes fought at their side and repelled pursuers. The pirates took their families and valuables along with them and, under the protection of

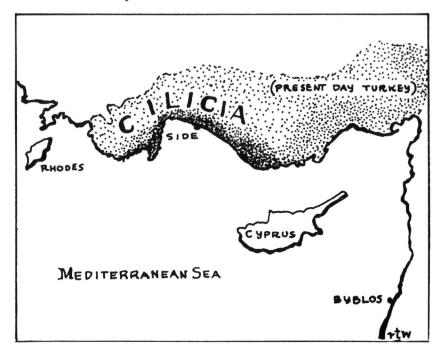

Cilicia, the greatest pirate stronghold in the Mediterranean during the first century B.C.

the inland warriors, remained until they could safely return to the coast.

After the fall of Rhodes the Cilician pirates began to organize enormous fleets of ships for raiding on land and for pirating at sea. They combined these fleets and formed a regular navy with home bases from which they operated. Recruits for their pirate ships came from all the maritime areas of the Mediterranean. The Cilician pirates sailed in regular squadrons under appointed commanders and admirals, and used their small, swift, open vessels in all areas of the Mediterranean. Since they considered themselves to be citizens of a legitimate state, they considered their plunder spoils of war. They even had client states among the Greek maritime cities who used their pirate fleets in times of war; they openly visited the slave market at Delos and traded; and they established the city of Side as their own trade center with its own slave market. At Side, and in other Cilician coastal cities, the pirates were freely allowed to use the docks to build their ships, and to organize their raiding expeditions.

The pirate depredations became so serious a threat to Roman commerce that the senate passed laws to contain their movements. One such law is especially interesting because it was such a notable failure. This law closed all the ports of the empire, and of allied states, to pirate vessels. It failed to accomplish anything more than to further consolidate the pirate forces in the Mediterranean. Under this law, passed about 100 B.C., the kings of Cyprus, Egypt, Cyrene, and Syria were ordered to "see to it that no pirate shall use your kingdoms, lands, or territories as a base of operations." The law's intent was to bring peace to the seas used by Rome, but it failed miserable.

Plutarch, the Greek writer who lived in Roman times, wrote a vivid series of biographies of emminent Greeks and Romans. In his life of Pompey he explained how the power of the Cilician pirates had begun.

> While the Romans were clashing in civil war, the seas lay unguarded . . . . Even wealthy men and nobles, supposed to have good sense, shared in the profits of piracy and sometimes in actual piratical adventures, as if such acts brought honor and distinction. So it may be understood why the pirates had anchorages and fortified beacon towers in many places, and their fleets were fitted for their piratical work with excellent crews, skilled pilots, and swift, light vessels.

He goes on to mention that there were music and dancing as well as carousal along every shore, and that "generals were kidnapped, and cities were captured and freed on payment of ransom. The pirate ships numbered over 1.000, and the cities taken and many of them ransomed . . . 400—all this, much to the disgrace of the Roman Empire."

Appian in his history of Rome says that the pirates "increased in number to tens of thousands. They dominated now not only the eastern waters, but the whole Mediterranean to the Pillars of Hercules, they also vanquished Roman generals in naval engagements . . . . Rome herself felt this evil most keenly, her subjects being distressed, and she suffering grievously from hunger."

In 74 B.C. the proconsul Marcus Antonius was given command of the navy and ordered to subdue the pirates. He occupied Cilicia for a time, but actually accomplished little. With his failure Roman discontent concerning the pirates grew more vocal, for Rome was now a trading nation and piracy could no longer be sanctioned. The busi-

Roman merchantman (from a marble relief at Ostia, ca. 200 A.D.).

nessmen of Rome were angry with the senate for doing little to subdue the pirates. The people of Rome were concerned because pirates were interrupting the shipments of grain to the city.

These were disturbed times when many strange things happened at sea. One of the most well-known incidents in the long history of piracy took place at this time when a young Roman sailed from Ostia intending to study political oratory with the famous teacher, Apollonius Molon, at Rhodes. When his vessel passed Pharmacusa, an island off the coast of present-day Turkey, pirates attacked and the passengers were captured. They did not think the young Roman was worth very much; attempting to settle on his ransom, they began by demanding a small sum. But, he thought highly of himself and insisted that they raise the amount by 250 percent. They readily agreed.

The captive was held for thirty-eight days, a very short time for such a transaction; some captives were kept in slavery for years while waiting the collection of ransom money. This particular captive was gregagious and spirited, so he joined the pirates in their games, entertained them by reading his literary compositions aloud, and when they didn't seem sufficitntly impressed, he called them nit-wits and ignorant barbarians. He also warned them that when he was free he'd find them and punish them as was fitting.

The story has various endings and seems embellished from beginning to end due to the fame the captive—Julius Caesar—later achieved. Some say that when the ransom arrived Caesar sailed to Miletus, armed and manned a small fleet, and hunted the pirates who had captured him, eventually seizing them. Caesar then had their throats cut. It is said he did this to save his recent comrades the pain of the slow death of crucifixion. Others say he did crucify them and angered the cities that had contributed to the ransom, since they believed it was their right to execute pirates. (A Roman law stated that pirates must be punished as publicly as possible, serving as an example to others.)

Events such as the capture of Julius Caesar, and the even closer pirate raids on the seaboard of Italy itself, brought the wrath of the people to a fever pitch. The barricaded doors and fortified walls and towers of the villas in seaside resorts at such places as Naples and Cumae were attacked by pirates. Cicero, the best orator and most gifted writer of that period, tells of the theft from Misenum of the children of a consul. Children from the noblest families were being captured. Plutarch mentions pirate violence to the praetors Sextilius and Bellienus, and the kidnapping of the daughter of Antonius.

The ignominious invasion of the city of Syracuse on Sicily by the pirate chieftain, Pyrganio, caused havoc in the city and surrounding countryside. The attack on the very port of Rome, Ostia, during which pirates destroyed a Roman fleet, and plundered at will, was also humiliating. There are many accounts of the attack on Ostia. One tells of the raiders sailing into the Tiber, burning ships, and plundering. When they met no opposition, the pirates settled in comfortably, and took their time disposing of the spoils and of the inhabitants they had captured.

The anger that this attack aroused was not so much caused by the seizure of the goods and movable wealth of a rich trading center, but by the disgrace it caused Rome. The pirates had, within a few miles of Rome, shown their contempt for the city's power. Who was safe if Rome could not defend her own port? The people of Rome

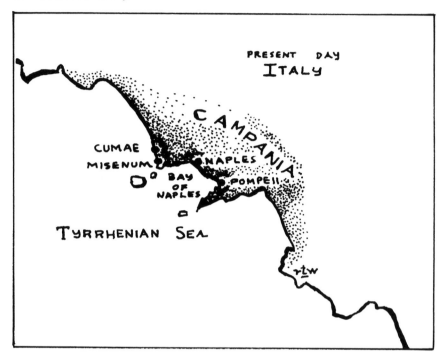

Campania, showing Naples and neighboring cities where wealthy Romans often had villas that were subject to pirate attack.

were furious with the senate for not having done more to suppress piracy. The result of this outrage and the angry response it caused was to produce one of the most efficient campaigns ever staged against pirates.

The operation began with a remarkable measure decreed by the Roman senators. Even today it is breathtaking in its grandness. A leader was to be appointed from the consuls; he was to take command for three years, and hold supreme sway over the entire Mediterranean, and all the coasts for fifty miles inland. He was to be able to dispose absolutely of all the resources of the provinces. Also, a large sum of money and a considerable force of men and ships were at once to be handed over to him. He was free to choose twenty-five lieutenants and two treasurers of senatorial rank to assist him. He was also given the special power to raise, in addition to the men and ships assigned to him initially, 12,000 infantry and 7,000 cavalry, and a fleet of 500 ships. To all practical purposes the government of Rome was put in the hands of the man chosen for this command.

Gnaeus Pompeius, later called Magnus, "the great," but known to us simply as Pompey, was given this sweeping authority in 67 B.C. He had served Rome in Sicily, Africa, and Spain where he had dealt with the pirates who had fixed stations along the coast there, and on his return to Rome he hunted down the fugitive slaves fleeing after the defeat of their leader Spartacus. His moderate and thoroughly organized approach to the problems facing him was the reason for his great success in the pirate war. Those who had preceeded him in the attempt to stop plundering had applied force at one point and then another, allowing the pirates time to send reinforcements to any section of the seas threatened by the scattered Roman fleets.

Pompey's solution to the problem of the flexibility of the pirate forces was simple: he divided the Mediterranean and Black seas into thirteen separate but unified commands, each with a group commander who equipped vessels, searched coasts, rounded up pirate forces, and destroyed their strongholds. This plan dealt a death blow to the hitherto mobile pirates, frustrating their attempts to join forces and achieve power through combined strength.

Pompey himself took personal command of 200 warships and seventy lighter vessels. With the best of these ships he swept through Sicilian, African, and Sardinian waters. Other forces in the west dealt with the coasts of Spain and Gaul. Within forty days the pirates in the western Mediterranean were defeated. Then, with sixty of his fastest ships Pompey sped east to Lycia and Cilicia. The Lycians, confronted with the powerful fleet, accepted the generous terms that Pompey offered them, and retired from the sea. He treated them with clemency, a practice not common in those times, and settled them in uninhabited or thinly peopled areas where they could support themselves by peaceful means. He showed great wisdom in not executing individuals indiscriminantly, thus preventing bitterness among the pirates and the return to their plundering ways.

Unlike the Lycians, the Cilicians decided to fight Pompey's forces. They secreted their treasures and families inland and with a powerful fleet waited for the Romans. With his well trained Roman soldiers and seamen, and the power of the Greek and eastern cities behind him furnishing ships and supplies, however, Pompey easily defeated the Cilicians at sea. Then he landed and subdued their strongholds, defeating the native tribes as well as the pirates. Only forty-nine days after his first appearance in the East the war came to a close. The achievement astounded the ancient world. Hundreds of vessels had been either captured or destroyed, over a hundred of the pirate cities, fortresses and other points of congregation were taken or destroyed; thousands of pirates were cleared from the sea, and perhaps as many as 10,000 killed in battle.

The words of Cicero concerning Pompey's actions still ring with Roman pride.

> All the pirates who were anywhere to be found were now either taken prisoner and put to death or else surrendered themselves voluntarily to the power and authority of this one man. And thus Pompey at the end of winter prepared, at the beginning of spring undertook, and by the middle of summer terminated this most serious war, which had lasted so long, which was so scattered in such distant and various places, and by which every nation and country had been incessantly distressed.

Strabo put it more succinctly: "Since the pirates have been suppressed, those who sail enjoy complete quiet in the present peace." With the end of the pirate war, trade flourished as never before: Ostia was avenged.

Although the Roman fleet assigned to the Syrian coast hampered further serious outbreaks by the Cilician pirates, piracy did not come to an end in the Mediterranean Sea. Pompey tried to continue the war against piracy by attempting to have a standing fleet inaugurated for sea patrol, but he was not successful in the attempt. He realized that Rome's Mauretanian fleet of about twenty liburnians stationed at the port of Caesarea in North Africa was too small to protect that coast and the coast of Spain; he knew that Roman fleets at Alexandria, Ravena, and elsewhere were under the control of Roman nobles who were often dishonest; and he saw that the fleets were built up or let fall into decay according to the urgency of the times. But Pompey was helpless, for the treasury of Rome was not in his hands, and the Romans followed the path at sea that they had from the beginning, the path of neglect. Thus Pompey's great campaign was not the end of piracy during the years of Rome's rule as it might have been.

The long war against the pirates had lasted for nearly half a century, the intensity increased as the years passed until the last ten years between 76–67 B.C. After Pompey's campaign against

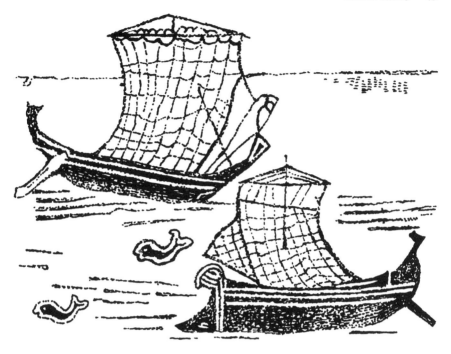

Roman merchantman and war galley. Mosaics of merchantmen accompanied by war galleys were common in ancient Rome, which may indicate that certain vessels frequently sailed under the protection of fighting craft. The lower vessel is the fighting ship, indicated by the ram at its bow (*left*). The upper vessel is the merchantman, with curved bow and stern.

them, pirates still supplied the slave market, and there were occasional large outbreaks of piracy such as that of the Jewish pirates who operated freely out of the port of Joppa (Jaffa). They were not suppressed until Rome defeated the Jews and captured that city. There were even pirate revolts, one, amazingly, led by Pompey's son, Sextus Pompeius, in 42 B.C. And in the early 30s B.C. the Illyrians once again began causing trouble with their acts of piracy at sea and on land. In 34–33 B.C. the emperor Augustus sailed against them, destroyed their strongholds on the coast and in the interior as well, and wisely followed up victory with colonization. For many years afterward the Adriatic, at least, was really cleared of piracy.

Some frontiers, however, were never fully secured against sea raiders. It was always necessary to have a strong Roman fleet in the Black Sea to protect the mouth of the Danube and other places in that area under Rome's dominance. In the time of Tiberius (A.D.

14-37) the pirates of the eastern coast of the Black Sea raided freely at sea, and also landed and levied taxes on the villages and towns of that region. In this area the pirates continued to raid and plunder; but Rome was powerful and they shrewdly avoided coming into contact with Roman troops on land. In spite of this piratical activity at the periphery of the empire, from the time of Augustus (30 B.C.–A.D. 14), to that of Septimus Severus (A.D. 193–211) there are few references to pirates in either Roman literature or histories.

When piracy did once again begin to increase it began in such places as the Black Sea and among the northern tribes, and here was an ominous sign. As these raids continued they became part of a great threatening migration of peoples toward the center of Rome. The barbarian plunderers, their maritime adventures beginning with small fleets, soon appeared with swarms of ships. By the fourth century the pirate ships at sea numbered in the thousands, and stealthy piratical voyages gave way to open attack. The days when Rome ruled the western world were coming to an end.

5. Piracy and the Fall of Rome

According to many historians who emphasize the part European nations have played in the history of man, little of importance happened in the world between the collapse of the Roman Empire of the West and the Age of Chivalry. In maritime histories especially, writers usually jump from the fall of Rome to the Norman invasion of England. The Dark Ages descended on Europe, the serf shivered in his hovel, and the barbarians of the Gothic world blotted out the old civilization built up by the Greeks and Romans. Travel is supposed to have nearly ceased because the roads were so poor and dangerous to use, and the seas so infested with pirates.

This telescoped view is unrealistic. Although civilization took a downward turn in the parts of the world held by the Western Roman Empire, there were stimulating and interesting developments in the Near East and elsewhere. The rise of the Eastern Roman Empire in Byzantium, and the growth of Islam, along with the developments in the Gothic, Italic, and British kingdoms are events well worth looking into, particularly with respect to piracy.

After Pompey's swift and successful campaign against the pirates of the Mediterranean, voyagers could usually travel unmolested from the islands of Greece to the Strait of Gibraltar. Augustus' reign, beginning in 31 B.C., ushered in two centuries of profound peace. The powerful Roman army so absolutely controlled the coasts of the Mediterranean that there was no necessity for a powerful navy to control pirates. Pirates need land bases from which to operate, and none was available on the shores of the Mediterranean. A brisk trade was carried on as the great "round" merchantmen went from Roman port to Roman port. Each of these vessels could hold several hundred passengers and hundreds of tons of cargo.

All the sea lanes in the Mediterranean, like all roads in the area, led to the peaceful and bustling city of Rome. There were splendid harbors everywhere. The emperor Tiberius Claudius (reigned A.D. 41–54) made Ostia into a stately and beautiful marine portal to the city. With little fear of pirates, a merchant could go from there to Athens in a week, or to Spain in the same length of time. A letter written by a Roman mother to her son serving in the army in Alexandria could be delivered in ten days or two weeks by ship. There was even a Roman fleet of over a hundred vessels that sailed from the Red Sea to India every year, returning with silks, perfumes, and other rare and valuable cargoes, such as diamonds from the secret mines of India, mines that no European had ever seen with the exception of Alexander the Great.

Often the "fall" of this great empire is pictured in dramatic fashion with barbaric hoards suddenly appearing at its boundaries. They are said to have swept down from the north, butchering and burning, and quickly devastating the civilized southern section of the continent. Or, without warning primitive and cruel pirates are said to have begun to ravage the coasts from the Black Sea to Spain. The truth of the matter, however, is more curious and startling.

Actually, neither the return of the pirate fleets nor the conquest of Rome by the Gothic tribes happened abruptly. Piracy came back to the Mediterranean world because the emperors of Rome ever so slowly ceded their power to Gothic leaders. Barbarians had played an important part in the history of the Roman army. When Julius Caesar conquered the Gallic areas covered by present-day France and Belgium (58–51 B.C.), his cavalry was largely made up of barbarians. Over the years the army became increasingly foreign, not only the enlisted men, but the officers as well. In A.D. 137 (six years after the great plague that decimated the population of Rome), barbarian Goths from the northern forests broke through the wall between the upper Danube and the upper Rhine. The enormous barracks and forts in this wall were already in charge of Rome's Gothic legions.

Concerned with the invasion from the north the emperor, Marcus Aurelius, decided that it was necessary to take the unusual step of establishing a large standing army. He sold the crown jewels to raise cash for equipping and supplying this army. When his money ran out and he was unable to raise the additional vast sums needed for the army, he turned to the barbarians and struck a bargain—if they joined the Roman army he would pay them in land on which they could settle. Whole tribes migrated over the borders, bringing their tribal customs, as well as their own Gothic leaders who became recognized as Roman officers. From that time onward the army of Rome was *mainly* composed of barbarians, or the children of barbarians. Although they took on the outward appearance of Romans, they remained Gothic in their habits and hearts. The wonderful era of peace ended, and the dominance of Rome by the less civilized Gothic tribes began.

The death of Marcus Aurelis (A.D. 180), and the rule of his weak and selfish son, Commodus, who squandered what was left of the imperial treasury, introduced nearly a hundred years of civil strife. There was no legal means of choosing an emperor, and the barbaric troops discovered that when an emperor died they could elect a new one, just as they did with their tribal kings. In the fifty years from A.D. 235 to A.D. 285 there were twenty-two emperors. Twenty of them were murdered, a reflection of the anarchy of the times. And, more and more, the troops in the provinces set up separate emperors of their own.

At sea the situation was as bad. Here Rome was a peaceful trading empire, not a warring empire as on land. When piracy began to increase at the periphery of the empire, there was no strong naval force to check it. In the east, the natives of the Black Sea region began to raid, penetrating further and further along Roman shores. At first they did not stay in the areas they raided because they feared the Roman troops; instead they returned home laden with rich booty. Their first large scale attacks began in the mid-250s. The most successful were undertaken by the Goths, who took to the sea at Tyras at the mouth of the Tyras (Dniester) River in what is now Russia. As they went along they captured fishing vessels and other craft. Slowly they plundered their way to the province of Bithynis on the southern shore of the Black Sea. Here they ravaged four important cities. So savage were these continuing pirate raids, and the raids of other barbarians in the region, that the trade of the Black Sea was disrupted.

In the year 267 the Goths and other tribes of the east began to penetrate the Aegean. In that year a large fleet—some historians of that era say it was composed of as many as 500 ships—sailed out of the Black Sea and into the Bosphorus. Suddenly it appeared before the shocked city of Byzantium. But even in surprise the city was strong enough to resist the pirates, and forced them to sail on and pillage elsewhere. They sailed into the Aegean and sacked Athens, Corinth, Argos, and Sparta. But, on the pirates' voyage back to the Black Sea the people of Athens, with the support of a Roman squadron, laid an ambush and killed many of the raiders. It was only a momentary set-back for the pirates, however; in 269 the Goths put together a fleet of 2,000 ships and entered the Aegean again. They boldly blockaded the port of Thessalonica, one of the greatest harbors in the eastern Mediterranean, with a part of their fleet. The remaining vessels went on to raid along all the coasts of the east, as well as the islands of Cyprus and Crete. With this action simple pirate raids began to give way to invasion from the sea by the Goths.

In the north, too, with the disintegration of the central government of Rome, Frankish and Saxon pirates of the lower Rhine became increasingly active. In 286 the Roman fleet at Gessoriacum (now Boulogne) was ordered to force as many of these pirates off the sea as possible. The fleet was put under the command of Carausius the Menapian, who was probably a Belgian. To curb the pirates Carausius adopted an unorthodox policy. He allowed them, apparently, a free hand. Any who wanted to leave port to raid could do so. It was only on their return, when they were loaded with rich booty, that the commander's fleet went into action, intercepted the vessels, and captured the plunder for Carausius.

Carausius, who historians of the day called "dark and mysterious," quickly accumulated a great fortune. In the meantime his actions were learned of in Rome, and his death was decreed. When news of the death sentence reached him, the commander solved the problem by bribing the Roman soldiers, as well as the Franks and Saxons, to proclaim him emperor. He sailed his fleet to Britain and

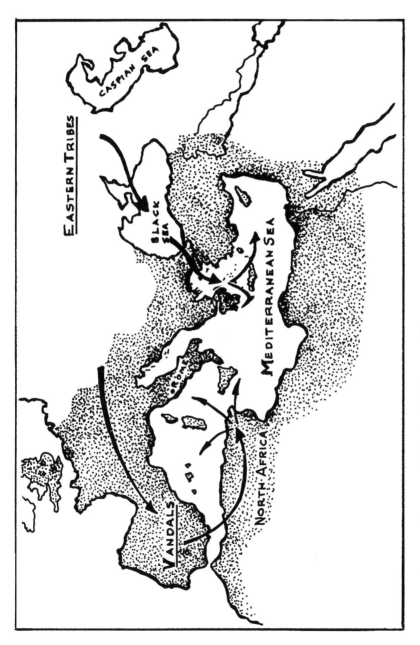

Eastern and western pirate routes during the declining years of Roman power.

became its ruler. (It was often as simple as that in those disordered times.) Rome, faced with an accomplished fact, came to terms with the commander, and granted him recognition. The surprising condition for this recognition was that Carausius should keep the seas of the north free of pirates—a condition he did not keep. Rome formed another fleet, and by 298-9 the northern pirates were defeated at sea. They were settled in northeast Gaul, and commerce began to flourish again on the seas of the area.

The fleet that Carausius had taken over was called the *Classis Britannica*. It had been a standing force for many years, with the duty of protecting both coasts of the Strait of Dover. Rutupiac (Richborough) was its British port, and from there and Gessoriacum (Boulogne) flotillas were sent out to police and sweep the coasts. After the defeat of the pirates this flotilla functioned successfully for years, until the middle of the fourth century when Jutes, Saxons, and Angles began raiding in force again.

These tribes had engaged in piratical activities since the second century. At first these barbarian pirates avoided Britain, possibly because of the new coastal defense system set up there called the Saxon Shore. But, by the early 340s Britain became their major target. By the early 360s Rome was loosing its control of Britain. The island was slipping back into a primitive condition. Wanting to save it for the Empire, Theodosius—one of the greatest of Roman generals—went there to restore order. Although he succeeded in destroying many of the raiders, he then left. Such unsubstantial and temporary aid from Rome was not significant and by 383 eighty-five Roman cities and villas had been abandoned. Coastal forts were kept in repair, but manning them was difficult. There simply were not enough Romans to deter the raiders.

The troops of Rome were withdrawn early in the 5th century (407), and a few years later a great concentration of pirates on the sea surrounding Britain indulged in massive pillaging and burning. Romanized Britains fled, and Gildas, a British historian, wrote, "The country was harried far and wide, the cities spoiled, and the inhabitants slain or enslaved." The brief golden age of Romanized Britain came to an end, and for the next 600 years some of the most brutal scenes in the history of man were played out along the shores of the British islands.

Thus piracy increased as Rome splintered. In the fourth century the novels of Roman writers swarmed with pirates, reflecting actual conditions. Even books on such subjects as the social graces touched on piracy. Macrobius, a writer who appears in 395, described "how to carry on a conversation so that your guests will tell you of their brilliant deeds," for example, "how, when the whole fleet was boarded by pirates, they alone by their cunning or their valor escaped."

More important than the loss of Britain or the pirate raids in the east was the appearance of the Vandals in North Africa. Under King Gaiseric, called the Lame, 80,000 Vandals migrated from Spain to North Africa in May of 429. In the first year after the conquest of the Roman provinces in western North Africa, Gaiseric took possession of the small fleet of swift cruisers maintained at Carthage to protect the coast against pirates. He formed pirate fleets, and Carthage (adjacent to modern Tunis) became a pirate stronghold. Thus the Vandals established a kingdom the power of which was based on the strength of its pirate fleets.

On or near the coasts Rome's richest cities flourished. With continuing pirate raids against Sicily, Calabria, and other parts of the Italian peninsula, the sea lanes of the empire were subject to costly disruption. Raw materials, manufactured goods, and grain supplies could no longer move freely in the Mediterranean. Pirate raiding on land and sea by Gaiseric's seamen, and the piratical inroads to commerce, severely curtailed the development of manufactured goods and of the resources of the western Mediterranean. The Roman Empire was being split at sea; the existence of the Empire was threatened.

With each passing decade that they controlled the seas, the Vandal pirates went further and further afield. By 440 they were attacking Sicily and Sardinia in force, moving about freely and creating terror by burning and pillaging; to all intents and purposes they, not Rome, were in control of these islands. A definite split had already taken place in the Empire in 284 when the Emperor Diocletian went to live at Nicomedia (just to the east of Byzantium) where he could direct the almost continual wars with New Persia. To attend to the western part of the Empire he appointed an emperor at Rome. Although Constantine (reigned 324–337) did not intend to

The Sea of Marmara, connecting the Black Sea and the Aegean. The city of Byzantium was called Constantinople from A.D. 330 to 1930, when it was re-named Istanbūl.

divide the empire, that was the end result when he established a new capital at Byzantium on the European side of the Bosporus. (It was renamed Constantinople after him. The Arabic form of the emperor's name is *Stambūl,* from which the Turkish form of Istambūl is derived.) Now, added to the physical and political split, came the commercial split.

The activites of the pirates threatened the Italian peninsula, which relied on the islands of Sicily and Sardinia for grain. Famine loomed if the pirates were not curtailed. The emperor of West Rome decided he had to have relief, otherwise all Italy might be destroyed. Thinking to bring peace by compromise and reward, the Emperor awarded King Gaiseric of the Vandals sole and complete rule of western North Africa in 442—and the Romans there now became a subject people. With this act another chunk of the Empire was lost.

Still the Vandals did not cease their piratical activity. By June of 455 they had achieved such power at sea that they were able to land at the port of Rome, and march on the city. They met no resistance, stayed two weeks and left with all the treasure of the city they could haul or carry. The imperial palace was sacked, as well as the temples. There was no slaughter, and no firing of buildings, only the taking of plunder and prisoners, many of whom were ransomed.

In 456 a strong Roman general, Ricimer, who was the actual ruler of the west, defeated a Vandal fleet off Corsica, and there was much rejoicing in the city and along the coasts. (Ricimer was pure Goth—it was he who elected puppet emperors who were Roman.) But, the next year, using Spain as his base, Gaiseric surprised the Roman fleet, captured its ships, and re-established Vandal power at sea. For the next twelve years there was such a reign of terror at sea, the Vandals going as far as Greece, that Goths and Romans united in raising a great fleet to combat piracy. The object was the capture of Carthage, the base used by most of the pirates operating in the western Mediterranean. Gaiseric calmly waited for the Roman fleet to gather before the port. He sent messages to the Romans saying they should not be hasty, that there could be a peaceful settlement to the matter through negotiation. Then, when the Roman leaders rowed ashore for the talks, the Vandals sent fire ships among the mighty Roman armada and destroyed most of it.

While the Vandal pirates sapped the commercial strength of the Western Roman Empire, the Eastern Roman Empire grew strong and rich. Its Oriental splendor was not the effete and fragile sort so often mistakenly attributed to kingdoms and rulers in this tumultuous region of the world. The power of Byzantium was backed by a strong army and by a mighty navy that controlled the Bosporus, the eastern Mediterranean, and the Black Sea. This well-ordered navy protected the shipping of the eastern Roman world from Constantinople to Alexandria. It nurtured Greek ports, and policed the waters surrounding the many Greek islands.

In 533–4 the emperor of the east, Justinian, sent an armed fleet under the brilliant leadership of his general, Belisarius, to destroy the Vandals who were still causing turmoil along Mediterranean shores. Methodically Belisarius cleared them from Sicily, Sardinia, and the Italian peninsula itself. He was wildly cheered in Rome and offered the crown of Italy, which he declined. His campaign in Italy and North Africa was the beginning of the conquest of the Mediterranean by the Byzantine (Eastern Roman) Empire. Within the next twenty

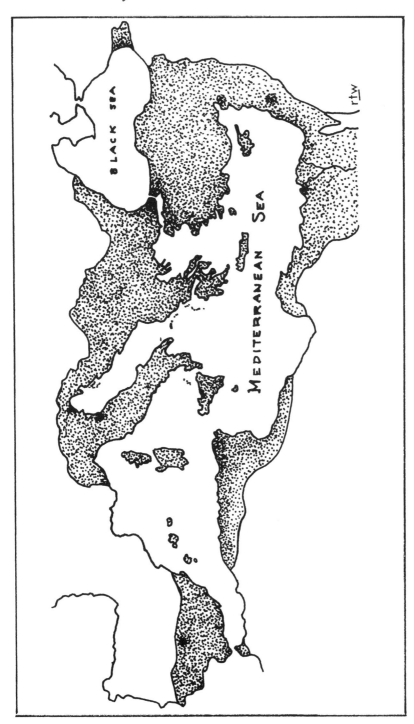

Byzantine Empire, mid-500s.

years the Byzantine navy was successful at suppressing piracy and bringing order to the coasts. The Byzantines could not control the large land masses in the west as the earlier Romans had done; but with swift armed galleys they patrolled the seas, and with these efficient patrols nearly a century of peace on the waters of the Mediterranean followed. The supremacy of the Byzantine navy was not challenged until the rise of the Arab navies in the 600s.

6. Moslem and Latin Pirates

Long-distance trade continued from 200 to 700, even when the Vandals were at their peak. Throughout this period Syrian traders continued to carry luxury goods as far as the European shores facing the Atlantic. Silk, spices, papyrus, and gold continued to flow to the coasts of Belgium, France, and Spain when the barbarians replaced the Romans. The formation of fleets of Arab pirates, however, marked the end of this trade, and after 700 Eastern luxuries virtually disappeared from the barbarian courts of Europe.

In Europe from the early 700s to 1800s the image of the feared pirate was an image of the Moslem pirate. In the Moslem states piracy developed as a way of life. During these centuries a good share of pirate booty (gold, goods, or slaves) went to the rulers of the Moslem states and added considerably to their treasuries. This came about because of the Moslem tribal traditions and religious views. Raiding and piracy were not considered morally wrong.

Before the 700s the Arabian peninsula and the Arabs in the surrounding areas were organized in small kingdoms. The inhabitants were mostly nomads who often lived as much by brigandage on land and sea as they did by herding. The sea route from India and the Orient followed the Arabian shores. With false signal lights and other ruses, and with small flotillas, the local tribes were adept at capturing shore-hugging vessels that traveled this route. On land, caravans made their way from the Persian Gulf to Damascus on the one side, or, if goods did not go by the dangerous Red Sea to Alexandria, other caravans carried them from Yemen through Mecca to the Mediterranean on the other side. There was no strong link between the northern Bedouin tribes and the southern Arabian kingdoms except a common poetic language. Judaised Arabs were common, as were Christian ones. The pre-Moslem Arabs were mostly pagan, however, and worshipped three important Gods and a higher Supreme God, or "Al-ilah."

Early in the seventh century Muhammad, the prophet of Islam (which means submission to Allah, and from which comes the word Moslem), appeared. Faith in Allah and his prophet replaced the old pagan beliefs. With great speed and intensity the small Arab groups were incorporated into a powerful Islamic community under Muhammad, and after him under his successors, called caliphs. A great movement in history had begun, and its leader, Muhammad, himself led raids on merchant caravans. Such raids were considered legitimate, and the booty from them a sign of divine favor. Previously the aim of such raids on land and sea had been simply piracy or robbery, but with the birth of Islam their avowed aim was to rid Arabian territories of Jews and Christians.

With the death of Muhammad (June 8, 632) greater Arab unification took place, and the age of Islamic conquest began. By 633 Syria and Iraq were brought into the Islamic sphere, in 639 Egypt (although Alexandria did not surrender to the Arabs until 641), and in 644 Mesopotamia. With the capture of Alexandria, the second most important port in the Byzantine Empire, the Arabs had an important naval base from which they could control the sea routes over which grain for Constantinople was carried. And, from the ports of Syria it was not long before small flotillas of pirates expanded into fleets of pirates operating with official approval.

One of the greatest pirate wars in history now began with unnumerable Moslem raids at sea and along the coasts of the Mediterranian. Only occasionally during the next centuries were there truces and exchanges of prisoners. Pirate raids at sea, as well as along the shore, preceded the Moslem conquest of North Africa and of the islands of the Mediterranean. In 649 Cyprus was taken, and Rhodes ravaged by Moslem pirates. More significant, a few years later a good part of the Byzantine fleet was destroyed. North Africa was consolidated under Moslem rule by 708—the date, probably, when

Syrian merchants ceased to trade with Belgium and other places beyond the Strait of Gibraltar. Shortly afterward (711) the Arab-Berber tribes of the west began the conquest of Spain.

Under the leadership of a Moslem Berber named Tarik, their first step was the conquest of a mountain at the entrance of the Mediterranean. It was given the name Tarik's mountain, or *Jabal Tarik*—Gibraltar. The conquest of Spain (al-Andalusia, or land of the Vandals), was encouraged by the pirate raids of 710 which were so successful and so easy for the Moslems. Such enormous and valuable booty was taken on these raids that the Berbers could not resist attacking Spain in force. On French and Italian shores the Moslem Berber pirate attacks continued for centuries. But the Moslems also carried on a peaceful trade with Christian Europe, though on a small scale; their trade with the Orient was more important to them. (The trade with Christians went on despite a prohibition against it by the Roman Church.) But, generally, Moslem leaders encouraged piracy against Christian Europe, rather than commerce. (As will be seen later, the Christian countries followed the same policy—the encouragement of piracy.) By the 800s Moslem pirates were reaping enormous rewards. They became too successful, too great, and too important to be stopped even by Moslem leaders.

Moslem forces captured Crete from Byzantium early in the ninth century, and Crete became a nest of corsairs[1] who ravaged the Aegean. In 828 two Byzantine expeditions were dispatched to dislodge the Moslems, but both failed. When his fleet was taken by surprise, the Byzantine commander was captured and crucified, and his troops and his ships were completely annihilated. The capture of Crete was symptomatic, for by the 800s piracy was not enough, the Moslems were beginning to itch for the conquest of Christian lands, and they began to establish themselves on islands as a preliminary to greater raids. Pirates from the Moslem world had begun harassing Sicily in the mid-600s. By 902 all Sicily was under Moslem control.

---

[1] "Corsair" was originally derived from the medieval Latin word *cursa* or *cursus* (see Oxford Universal Dictionary) which meant a run, and eventually came to mean a hostile excursion or plunder. "Corsair" now means a pirate, a privateer, or a fast vessel used for piracy.

It became a pirate base from which the Moslems plundered and terrorized the whole Italian peninsula.

Sicily and other islands in the western Mediterranean fell to the Moslem pirates because there was not a naval power in the area strong enough to effectively resist them. By the mid-800s Sicily was remote from the main sources of Byzantine strength, and it was neglected by Roman emperors of the East. Bazil I, for example, who reigned 867–886 and who founded the Macedonian Dynasty, used the Byzantine fleet to transport materials for building churches instead of for defending Sicily.

Later emperors of the East were afraid of having a truly powerful navy which might become a weapon in dissenting hands and be used against them. They also feared the accumulation of great riches in private hands, especially among shipowners. The emperors decreed laws that hindered the formation of powerful shipping groups.

Thasos, a large island off the coast of Macedonia, became a Moslem pirate base in 866, and remained a pirate fortress for another hundred years. Another was at the mouth of the Garigliano River between Rome and Naples, a strategic location that allowed the pirates to plunder the abbey of Monte Cassino and to force Rome to pay them tribute. From a pirate nest at Garde Frainet on the extreme north coast of Italy the Moslems struck far inland, robbing and holding for ransom travelers as far away as the Alpine passes. The power of the Moslem pirate fleets that operated from such bases was demonstrated many times. In 904, for instance, Leo of Tripoli, a renegade from Byzantium, took Thessalonica after a three-day seige. With his efficient band, he not only took a vast amount of treasure, but captured 30,000 prisoners.

Although the clash between the Moslem states, Byzantium, and the Christian states of Europe was predominantly maritime and piratical in nature, peaceful trade did continue in the Mediterranean. In the early 800s the geographer, Ibn Khurradādheb, tells of merchants of the south of France who ". . . travel from west to east and from east to west . . . by land and sea. They take ship from Frank-land [France] . . . and land at Farania [just east of Alexandria]." He also mentions that they sometimes went to Antioch. The Mediterranean, in spite of pirates, was a very busy place with a great deal of local shipping and much direct long-distance trade. The profits were huge on such shipping ventures; they were well worth the risks involved. One Moslem merchant of that time explained in a letter that his losses at sea were great, but he was thankful that he had made a profit many times over the amount lost. Another merchant wrote, "Losses on the sea are made good quickly, if God wills it."

Early in the century before the new millenium, Byzantine fleets began to re-establish control of the shores of the eastern Mediterranean. It began with a spectacular triumph over the Moslem pirates who were led by the intrepid Leo of Tripoli. The improved recruiting and organization in the Byzantine navy, as well as the use of the deadly Greek fire,[2] helped repulse the Moslems at sea.

While the Byzantines were regaining control of the sea from the beginning of the 900s, new competitors, the Italian cities, began to gain power in the Mediterranean.The city of Venice had never completely severed ties with the Eastern Roman Empire. It was a protected and dependent Byzantine port and an important outlet of Byzantine wares in Europe. For centuries Greeks, Syrians, and other easterners had controlled the trade and ships used at the port. Gradually, beginning in the 900s, control of this trade came more and more under the sway of the Venetians themselves.

The city's peaceful trade with Byzantium induced the Ventians to build a strong naval force to protect shipping, ensure rich trading profits, and enlarge Venice's maritime domain in the Adriatic. With their navy the Venetians overpowered nearby competing cities. Piracy played a part in the city's history at this period, but more important was the policing of the Adriatic. Large and heavy warships were first constructed by Venice in the 800s. These vessels, called

---

[2] Greek fire was a combustable substance used against enemy vessels; the secret of how it was made was kept so successfully that even today no one is certain of its ingredients. Some historians think that it was composed of crude oil to which sulphur, pitch, or quicklime were added; others, that it was based on naphtha. In defending a port it could be spread on the surface of the water. Then it was ignited, kindling the attacking vessels which would be destroyed. It could also be put in earthenware containers, fused, lit, and hurled at the enemy. At sea, a tube device similar to the modern flame thrower was used.

Byzantine galley, 1100s.

chelandie (the term is general, for it applied to a number of different vessel types), were to protect Venice in case of attack by Moslem pirates who were active in the Adriatic at the time.

The policing of the Dalmatian coast by Venice is an interesting example of how, in various ways, a maritime power could deal with pirates. Piratical raids had originated on the Dalmatian coast for centuries. Rome solved the problem by conquest and settlement. Venice solved the problem by the use of naval force and diplomacy.

The busiest pirate base in Dalmatia was at the mouth of what is today called the Neretva River (in Yugoslavia). It was situated on a narrow bay, almost like a broad canal. At the head of this bay there were numerous islands, and these islands also were used as pirate bases.

As Venetian maritime power increased in the Adriatic it became necessary to deal with the Neretva pirates, as well as the pirates among the islands. The doges of Venice went to sea and fought naval battles against the pirate fleets. The doges themselves did not stay home and command from ornate thrones; they commanded at sea. (One doge was killed in a sea battle against the Neretva pirates.) Even after numerous engagements, however, Venice could not put an end to the Neretvas. Seeing this, the Venetians resorted to a sort of bribery for forty years: they gave gifts to the Neretvas, and bought slaves in the area. This succeeded in curtailing the piratical activity in the region. The city also established trading centers on the Dalmatian coast.

The Neretva pirates were content, for trade brought them more certain profits than piracy and was less dangerous. They took to peaceful trade so successfully that they became serious competitors of the Venetians, sometimes going out in fleets that rivalled those of Venice in number. As their maritime strength increased they grew wealthy, and became even more of a threat to Venice's commercial domination of the Adriatic.

In the year 1000 the doge of Venice, Pietro II Orseolo, formed a mighty fleet. The Venetians sailed forth and caused havoc along the Dalmation coast. Still, they failed to subdue the Neretva whose stronghold at the mouth of the river proved unassailable. However, by chance the Venetians captured nearly half a hundred Neretva merchants whose ships were loaded with valuable cargo. With these hostages they were able to force the Neretvas at the mouth of the river to come to terms. This accomplished, they were able to destroy the pirate strongholds on the islands at the head of the bay. Never again did the pirates of the Dalmatian coast have the stomach to face a Venetian war fleet.

The story of the Neretva pirates, like that of the Venetians, is a capsule history of most maritime powers. In their early development piracy was as important as, even more important than, peaceful commerce. Pisa and Genoa and other Italian cities became rich and powerful from the profits of their piratical activities and their eastern trade. Such cities were themselves continually subject to piratical raids by the Moslems.

In 1015 the Moslem ruler of Denia in North Africa sent fleets to raid along the European coast. With an armada of about 120 ships he attacked Sardinia, took considerable plunder, and captured many inhabitants to be sold as slaves. At this point the combined fleets of Pisa and Genoa, which had joined forces to repel the Moslems, appeared on the scene, engaged in a fierce battle with the North Africa pirates, and won a surprising victory. They drove the Moslems all the way back to the African coast.

Now a most natural development took place. The Genoese and Pisans, who previously had worked craft that were nothing more than miserable raft-like platforms, began to build up their maritime forces. They then took to the water as sea-going pirates themselves, attacking Moslem shipping, and even Moslem cities. Revenge against

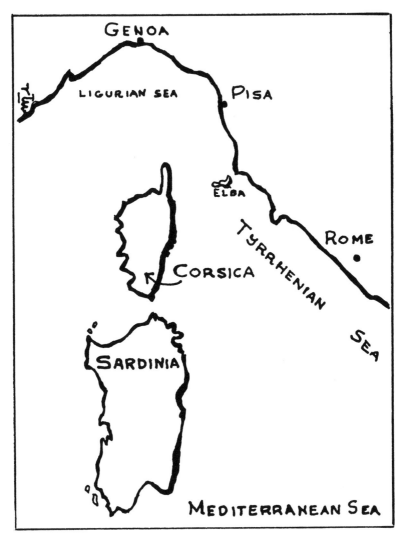

Area north of Rome, showing the location of Genoa and Pisa, cities that first became rich and powerful primarily from the profits of their piratical activities.

the Moslems, combined with a desire for wealth, motivated their raids during the eleventh century. Along with piracy, however, they took to trade, and many of the inhabitants of their cities turned to respectable commercial pursuits. Soon the Latin maritime powers not only gained control of southern Italy and Sicily, but also the coasts of Palestine and Syria.

By the time Christian Europeans seized Malta in 1090, many of the trade routes of the Mediterranean were already in Latin control. Eventually the sea was divided with the southern shores in the grip of the Moslems, and the northern coasts under the firm control of the Latins. The Moslems also controlled the waters around the Spanish

Europeans often depicted the tortures they underwent when captured by the Moslems. That European pirates and privateers also tortured prisoners was not often mentioned. Prints such as this one were used as propaganda to induce hatred of the Moslems.

peninsula, including the Balearic Islands (Majorca and others). The Byzantines ruled the eastern extremity of the sea, and much of the Black Sea. The war between these maritime powers took the form of continual pirate raids on sea and land.

The motives behind these skirmishes were primarily conquest and plunder. There was also the religious issue. "Christian dog" and "Mohammedan pig" were epithets tossed about with much verve and sincerity. Christian pirates were every bit as ruthless and cruel against other Christians, however, as they were against Moslems, and vice versa, so religious differences had little effect on piracy.

In this pirate war that lasted so many centuries the Europeans had two advantages; their bases were ideally situated to encourage maritime development, and they had cultivated other interests besides piracy. Commerce was of equal importance to both sides, but since the Europeans were in control of many of the important trade lanes, and had the strength and cunning to protect them, the Moslems were at a disadvantage. Italian, French, and northern European towns were developing during this period, and in such towns European maritime supremacy evolved. Industrial production grew also and European trade centers rapidly expanded.

Piratical activities of the Moslems, Norse, and others caused such centers to be fortified and strong commercial fleets to be built. The sustaining power, the continual aggressive drive, the intelligent development of arms, and the readiness to improve their vessels, especially their merchant fleets, were the hallmarks of subsequent European maritime power. Also characteristic was the support that local governments and the church gave to Christian pirate fleets; vast sums were spent equipping their corsairs.

An interesting feature of the continual war between traders and pirates in the Mediterranean at this time, and until after the 1400s, was the ships they used. The Venetian and Genoese galleys were based on Byzantine models, descendents of galleys of ancient times. The Byzantines called their warships *dromons,* which simply means runner. Of their *dromons,* the most widely used were the *direma.* These were of various sizes, some needing only 100 rowers, and others using as many as 300 men to work the oars. Another vessel they used was a faster one called a *birema,* a two-banked galley that was probably an adaption of the liburnium. These vessels also had sails; but sails were not used during combat, which was a hand-to-hand encounter between rowed warships. The Moslem *ghurāb* was a light galley that was propelled by about 140 oars. "Barges"—that is, flat-bottomed boats used for hauling—were open vessels, often sea-going, that carried cargo and passengers. Such "barges" often accompanied larger vessels on trading missions and acted as transports to and from trading stations that did not have well-developed port facilities.

Smaller and faster ships in support of larger ones used by the sea rovers often made the actual attack while the larger vessels stood off. Coastal pirates are described in Byzantine records of this period as raiding in small boats. Such small craft had been used in ancient times, and later also; a report in 1795 states that: "Boats of this sort, here called *trattas,* abound in every creek; they are long and narrow like canoes; then, twenty or even thirty men, each armed with a rifle and pistols, row with great celerity, and small masts with Latine [lateen] sails are also used when the winds are favourable."

Both European and Moslem merchant vessels plying the trade routes were similar to earlier "round" Greek and Roman ships, but they differed from the ancient ships in that they carried a lateen sail. The lateen is a triangular sail rigged fore-and-aft, in contrast to the square sail which is rigged from side to side. From ancient times the main sails on Mediterranean vessels were depicted as square, probably without exception.

With a lateen sail, a vessel is more easily maneuvered than with a square sail, for the lateen makes fuller use of the wind. The history of the development of the lateen mainsail is a mystery; no one can be sure when it was introduced into the Mediterranean. Arab literature of the 9th and 10th centuries describe a mainsail that, when seen from a distance, appeared like the fin of a whale; this seems to indicate that such sails were lateen. Some Byzantine ships are also shown in manuscripts in the 800s to be lateen-rigged, though others were square. The Moslems probably introduced the lateen into the Mediterranean from the Orient.[3]

---

[3] Some scholars believe that the lateen sail actually originated in the Mediterranean in Roman times. While it is certainly true that the Romans sometimes used two small triangle-shaped sails rigged above the yard on the

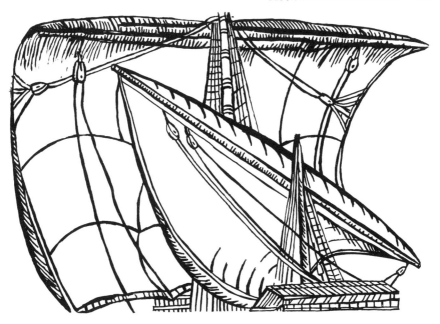

Lateen and square sails on a vessel.

Reports of the size of pirate fleets varied and were rarely dependable. In one instance there were reports that a merchant fleet was attacked by 200 galleys; the facts reported by a witness fortunate enough to escape were that he counted only ten. Pirate fleets put together for land raids often numbered around 100 vessels, but sometimes as many as 200 craft were sighted, both large and small vessels. Such numbers would be necessary if attack, especially of a fairly large port, was to prove effective. On the sea, however, flotillas were most likely to be used to overwhelm single merchantmen, and to cut merchantmen out of a convoy. Such flotillas attempted to cause so much devastation that single ships could be easily cut out and boarded during the confusion of the attack. This often allowed the other ships in the group or convoy to escape.

---

mainmast, these two small three-cornered sails were secured from one side of the vessel to the other, not fore-and-aft: they did not work with the wind, but were stationary. The trianglar mainsail on the mainmast came into general use in the Mediterranean sometime near the close of the first thousand years after the birth of Christ; no one knows where it originated. An "educated" guess would be the Pacific or the Indonesian archipelago.

Pirates at sea were sometimes beaten off. A Moslem source tells of twenty-seven Genoese galleys attacking a convoy of merchantmen and being driven away. In the early 1100s a Spanish ship setting out for Tunisia defended itself against an attack by pirates and made port safely.

As in Roman times merchant ships carried as many as 500 passengers, and there are records indicating that the number reached over 1000, and sometimes over 2000. Space was divided into that for men and for women, a man being entitled to three times as much room as a woman. (Men carried more equipment and also arms.) Passengers were not permitted to chop wood nor allowed to use their own fires to cook food, because of the danger of fire. A captain had a right to abandon a passenger on land if he had reason to, that is if the passenger caused disturbances or proved to be a thief. (This had been a captain's right from ancient Egyptian times.) He also had the

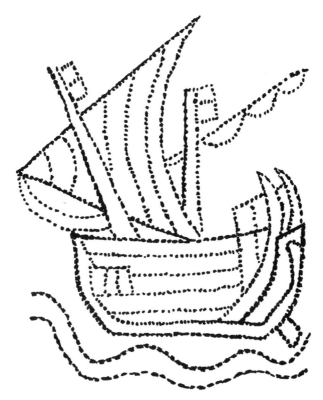

Italian merchant vessel of the 1000s.

right to jettison cargo if he thought it advisable during rough or stormy weather, or to lighten the vessel if the ship was pursued by pirates. The bales of cargo were intentionally made small and light, about 200 pounds, so that they could be heaved overboard with ease.

The enormous passenger capacity of these vessels, both Moslem and European, was a great inducement for pirates to attack. Slave markets were in operation in both the Moslem and Christian worlds, in Leghorn in Italy, and in Malta, Venice, Algiers, Constantinople, and other cities. Enslavement of pagans and Moslems was approved by the Roman Christian church, as well as the enslavement of the Christians of the Byzantine Empire, who were considered heretics. Slavs, Angles, Saxons, and other people were regularly bought and sold in the Christian world. Such slaves were used for domestic work, for agricultural work, or for mining and other rough labors; they were not used on galleys during this period. Rowers on galleys were free men, for oarsmen were also fighters, and slaves were not entrusted with military duties. (In the Moslem world slaves were permitted to engage in combat. Slavs, as well as men from the mountains around the Caspian Sea were welcome additions to Moslem troops.) Not until the 1600s and into the 1700s were "galley slaves" used in any number, for by the seventeenth century armament at sea was well advanced and rowers on galley did not have to fight. Cannon supplemented the sword in most serious engagements, although hand-to-hand fighting was still often the deciding factor.

As in ancient times capture by pirates meant great hardships. Ransom was possible, and was individualized at so much per person according to the captive's estimated value. The ransom demand increased if a captive was believed to have business connections or money available at home. Such people were often sold to a middleman for as much as a hundred pieces of gold. The middleman demanded what he thought the captive's family, friends, or business associates would pay for his release. Ransom negotiations for especially important captives, such as a governor or bishop, were carried out directly with the government concerned. Such ransom was often so steep that cities, provinces, and sometimes even countries were taxed heavily to raise it. In the Moslem world there was a standard ransom of only a few dinars for an individual on the lowest rung of the social ladder, the laborer.

Beatings and torture, sometimes causing death, were common for captured prisoners. Women and boys were sometimes raped, although in the case of younger women there was restraint, for the ransom, if any were to be paid, would be higher if no sexual abuse had taken place. The threat of such abuse was often used to squeeze more money out of a distressed family.

Pirates worked hard for their money, and during the winter months, when shipping ceased on the sea generally, pirates often led boring lives. At such times vessels were repaired and the time was passed in safe but dreary harbors or coves playing cards, drinking, cooking, and often, no doubt, arguing and fighting. Or a pirate returned to his home port or coastal settlement to visit his family, to make repairs to his home, to plant, fish, or do other domestic chores.

Success as a pirate required feats of seamanship not called for otherwise, except on naval warships. It was necessary to be aggressive, to search and strike. The compass and maps were coming into use and this allowed vessels more freedom of movement on the sea, but the majority of vessels stayed close to shore as they had in ancient times. The work was hard. Rowing long hours and fighting were not glamorous, nor were the endless hunt and the final chase.

Fire-throwers were used by the pirates of this era, as they were by the Byzantines during naval engagements, although Latins and Moslems at first did not know the secret of Greek fire. Before boarding, arrows and stones and other missiles were used. Bags of lime to blind, and sometimes flour, as well as soap or tallow to make decks slippery, were also hurled. Once aboard cutlass and dagger were brought into play.

The most well known weapon used by the Islamic pirates was a psychological one, their ululant cry—a violent, intense yell that sounded as if the demons of hell had been unloosed. (Oriental pirates used a similar cry.) During the Crusades many Europeans who had not heard it before were often unnerved and greatly impressed by the eerie quality of this Moslem battle cry.

Until 1182 the Latins and Byzantines were allied against the Moslems. Then, by a quirk of fate, conditions suddenly changed. In April of that year the famous "Latin Massacre" took place in Constantinople. Genoese, Pisans, and Venetians all had sections of the city set aside for their special use. During a rebellion early in 1182,

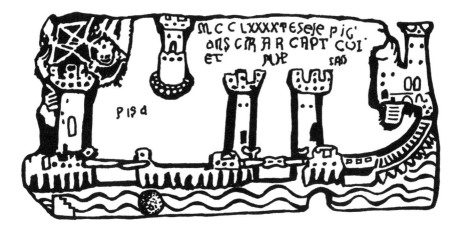

The port of Pisa as shown in a carving made in the 1200s. The barriers across the inner harbor's entrance were to prevent surprise raids by pirates.

mobs ravaged these areas killing many Genoese and Pisans. Forty-four galleys and many smaller ships filled with fleeing Latins managed to escape.

Seeking immediate revenge, the refugees, angered at the slaughter of friends and relatives and at their losses, raided Byzantine monasteries and towns on nearby coasts and islands. This was the beginning of a piratical plague of such brutality that the area did not fully recover for many years. What had begun as acts of revenge soon developed into the full-fledged business of piracy among the Genoese and Pisans. The Latin pirates began to attack all men at sea, not only the Byzantines. They killed and captured Venetians, Lombards, and other Latins, as well. They often used the subterfuge of friendship; they would come alongside their fellow Italians, then send a party to parlay, a common occurance at sea in all ages. Once aboard they would attack. Taken by surprise their fellow Latins were at a disadvantage. Letters and records of this time are filled with references to disguises used by pirates, the flying of false flags, and even the use of foreign vessels, both traditional ruses.

A strange feature of this pirate war was that often the Pisan and other Latin pirates were used by the Byzantines as part of their navy. They were also used to fight other Latin pirates. When the Genoese merchant Gafforio (or Caffaro) was arbitrarily fined by the Byzantines he got a fleet together to take vengence on the Aegean, raiding shipping lanes and cities. Imperial officials hired Giovanni Stirione, a Calabrian pirate, to fight him. Stirione was defeated and Gafforio was, for the moment, bought off with the promise of the governorship of a Byzantine province and gold.

Pisa and Genoa were then at war over Corsica, however, so the Emperor Alexius hired Pisan pirates to destroy Gafforio while negotiations were going on. Gafforio's pirate fleet was attacked and destroyed, except for four ships that escaped back to Italy; during the engagement Gafforio himself was killed.

The state of affairs was so confused and the damages from continued fighting were so severe that by the end of the century most of the Aegean islands were depopulated. The Cretans were attacking Genoese merchant ships are sea, the Genoese attacking the Byzantines, the Pisans the Genoese, and so on in a great roundabout of piracy. During the next few decades commerce might have been severely curtailed had it not been for the beginning of the Christian Crusades in 1096 which greatly increased the amount of shipping. Fighting men and pilgrims sailed from French, Italian, and Greek ports, shipbuilding saw an upsurge, profits were enormous and the losses from piracy were counterbalanced.

Greece and the Aegean islands, however, still suffered from rampant piracy for two reasons—the weakness of the Byzantine navy and corrupt government. Governors of the Greek provinces were not paid a regular salary; they were supposed to make their offices self-supporting. A tax, called ship-money, was levied on these provinces for the special purpose of suppressing piracy; but it was rarely used for that purpose; instead it went into the coffers of the governors. Frequently the governors also allowed pirates the use of ports in return for cash or a portion of their booty.

In the early 1200s when the Normans took over the control of Athens, they made little attempt to build a strong navy. The Latin pirates of the region, as well as local pirates, took advantage of this lack of sea-power. They preyed on shipping so much that a sail down the Gulf of Corinth was called "a voyage to Acheron," a fabled river in hell.

Because of these conditions the bishop of Thermopylae moved his residence inland, as others did. The fear of pirates was so great

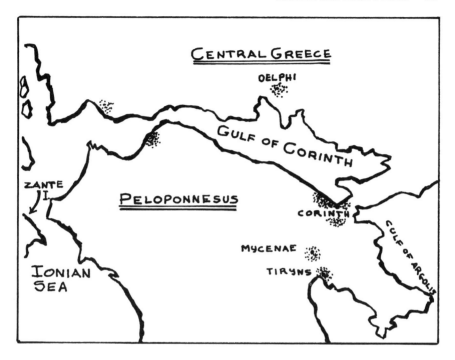

The Gulf of Corinth.

that people crowded together in fortifications for protection. The castle of the Crispi in the island duchy of Naxos was called a "pigstye" because of these crowded conditions; but nothing could be done to force the people to live in less crowded places. They believed that there was safety in numbers, although this did not always prove to be the case.

During the 1200's the pirates of the Moslem world mainly used the area between Barqa and Tobruk as a base. The Latins had bases on islands held by Latin nobles, especially among the Greek islands. Wherever there was a good harbor it was likely that pirate captains and their crews could be found. Piracy paid high dividends. A pirate venture was likely to be financed by the great and wealthy. The Lombard barons sailed a fleet of 100 ships every year to pillage along the coast of Asia Minor and at sea. The ruling families of Monemvasia in Greece, as well as the ducal family of Nauplin, boasted of their support of pirates and of their profits.

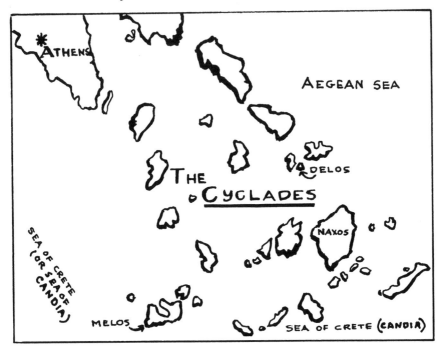

The Cyclades, where pirates, if captured, were roasted alive.

The cargo taken by these pirates was usually foodstuffs and slaves. Sometimes wine was taken, but seldom the strong, sweet wine of Morea called Malmsey, so favored by the feudal lords and ladies of the era; it usually sailed in fleets under special protection. Prisoners were sold into slavery, but often passengers and crews were killed out of hand, or sadistically mutilated (an act that would hinder sales if slavery were intended, but which, nonetheless, often took place). During the 1200s and 1300s many people of the Cyclades were sold into slavery by both Moslem and Christian pirates, in spite of the fact that these islands were increasingly fortified. The people of the area were so savagely against piracy that when a pirate was captured he was slowly roasted alive for hours. The penalty for pirates imposed by the Byzantine government was to blind them and then cut off their noses. A favored few, who might later be of use at sea, were sent to a special island prison from which escape was supposed to be impossible.

Piracy after the fall of Rome had helped to determine the formation and expansion of cities and of empires, and its appearance was often an early sign of the decay of a great power. It was in good part responsbile for the foundation of the great trading empire controlled by the Italian cities from 1100 well into the 1600s. In the late 1400s, however, the maritime world began to change rapidly with the oceanic advances of the Hanseatic League, France, Portugal, and Spain. These were the maritime peoples, along with the Dutch and the Italians, who were to mold the future of much of the world. After the discovery of the Americas the center of the western world shifted from the Mediterranean. Now men and ships sailing the great oceans were to shape future important events on land and sea.

7. Pirates of the North

Acts of piracy as bloody as any described in the ancient Greek epics were part of the conquest and colonization of new lands by the Norse—the people of Scandinavia. The adventures and raids of the people of the north, who freely roved the sea lanes of Europe between the end of the 8th century to the beginning of the 13th, form an important aspect of medieval history. From northern ships and maritime experiences Europe learned the fundamental lessons of oceanic sea power. With Norse ships Europeans launched their oceanic career, giving the continent of Europe dominance of the world's seas for hundreds of years.

Raiding and piracy were not new forces in the north, for, as we have seen, during Roman times piracy was common in the British Isles and along the coast of Gaul. Irish pirates, such as one with the picturesque name Niall-of-the-Nine-Hostages, went to sea in fleets of curraghs, which were vessels made of twigs bound together (withes or withies), sticks, and boards, all covered with hides. Such craft were light and flexible, and had been used for centuries by fishermen as well as pirates in many parts of the world. Long journeys, such as from Ireland to France or Iceland, were sometimes made in these vessels.

Niall was active during the late 4th century. Before and after him came many similar Irish pirates raiding such towns in Britain as Chester-on-the-Dee. Their primary aim was the capture of slaves for work in Ireland, although they also pillaged. One of the most popular stories concerning piracy is the capture of St. Patrick in the 400s by Irish pirates. After spending six years as a captive (about 405–411) the young man of Romanized British stock escaped to Gaul where he became a churchman, later returning to Ireland to preach in 432. In addition to Irish pirates, the inhabitants of Britain were plagued by pirates from the low coastal region that is now the Netherlands, who preyed on vessels plying between London and the continent. The pirates of Brittany, too, living in what is now northwestern France on land jutting out into the Atlantic, with the Bay of Biscay on one side and the Channel separating France and England on the other, were in a favorable position to attack passing vessels.

Piracy among the tribes of the Baltic, the "stormy and open sea" of the north, was noted by Roman writers. One Roman historian said the seamen of this area "excelled the rest of the people in their knowledge of nautical affairs." In the 8th century when piratical raids began to extend outside the Baltic three major groups were involved: the Danes, the Swedes, and the Norwegians. Little is known of their history before this time. The Norwegians were made up of Teutonic tribesmen who formed separate, strong, independent settlements headed by petty kings. At about the time of the first overseas raids there were some thirty of these small kingdoms in Norway. (Norwegian colonization of the northern islands off Scotland preceded the Viking Age by a few hundred years; the Norwegians used these islands as bases for their raids on the British Isles.) The inhabitants of Sweden were also Teutonic and separated into petty tribal kingdoms, as were the Danes who occupied the peninsula of Jutland and the adjacent islands in the Baltic Sea.

These people were joined only by their common pagan religious beliefs; they were not united. The terms Viking, Norseman, and Northman are simply used today for convenience. The countries that later became Norway, Denmark, and Sweden did not begin to have significant individual existences as kingdoms until the late 10th century.

In general, the Swedish traveled by river from the gulfs on the Baltic and raided through Russia and in the Black Sea. The Danes and Norwegians—probably the fiercest warriors amongst the Scandanavians were the Norwegians—raided the British Isles and areas that are present-day France, Germany, and the Netherlands.

Norse raiding routes.

The men who went on these raiding expeditions were often the most ambitious and talented, as well as the most lawless and unscrupulous. The leaders were often men who were royally born. The crews were made up of sturdy seamen and seasoned warriors. Young men of the royal and high-born families also went on such voyages, as part of their education. These men were not rowdy oafs; they were almost always well disciplined and shrewd. Much has been made of their inordinate fondness for strong drink—on occasion they had almost ceremonial bouts, drinking themselves insensible—but most people of the time did this, for strong drink was aspirin, tranquillizer, and conversation stimulant of the day. The milkmaid, as well as the duchess, began the day with a hearty mug of ale, and by nightfall many a head in the Middle Ages was nodding from weariness due to hard work and heavy drinking.

The saga of the Norse pirate raids is a complex one, for the Norse, unlike the Goths and other barbarian raiders, were not merely primitive herdsmen. During the late 700s and until the 1000s, when the Norse were most active on the sea, there was an expanding and healthy economy in the Scandanavian countries. Although much capital (accumulated wealth employed to produce more wealth) was tied up in trade, especially in Sweden, agriculture was developing at a greater rate than ever before. Simultaneously a large increase in population sent the raiders to sea in great numbers to search for land on which to settle. Due to the improved economic conditions, raiding within the Scandanavian countries themselves was more profitable than ever. The more powerful Norse kings or chiefs indulged in such raids and began to subdue their weaker rivals.

Conditions at home and abroad created an atmosphere conducive to lawlessness. The great Frankish empire of the Carolingian kings (751–987) quickly disintegrated with the death of Charlemagne in 814. It soon was separated into three weaker lands. Northern Europe was now ripe for the ravages of the Norse.

The usual center of people's lives at the time was the manor (villa—village) with its lord. On the manor, land and labor were organized for the production of agricultural products: flax and wool for making clothing; grain, beans, and livestock for food; barley and grapes for making ale, beer, and wine. The lord's dwelling was a fortress for armed horsemen employed to protect the peasants.

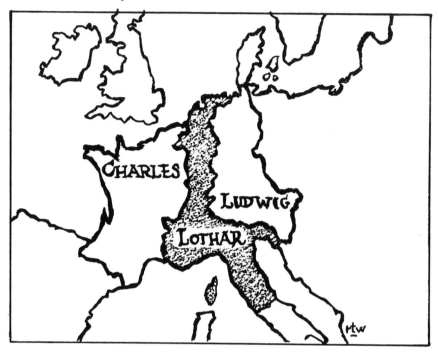

The division of the Frankish Empire, A.D. 843.

Castles arose on manor lands beginning in the late 800s. The earliest castles were simple blockhouses built solely of timber. Stone castles did not appear until late in the 1000s, and even then generally only the tower (called donjon or keep) was built of stone. Raids, private wars, and invasions were common, with horses often being kept in the rooms or halls where the nobles or fighting men slept so as to have them ready for defense at any time.

Into this world during the later part of the 700s the Norse suddenly appeared. Gibbon in his *Decline and Fall of the Roman Empire* states that for the Northmen, "Piracy was the exercise, the trade, the glory, and the virtue of the Scandinavian youth. Impatient of a bleak climate and narrow limits, they started from the banquet, grasped their arms, sounded their horns, ascended their vessels, and explored every coast that promised either spoil or settlement."

The impulse to raid was a natural one in the north. War and piracy were a normal profession of free Norseman; farming and building was work relegated to churls (serfs). To be at sea was also a normal activity for many Northmen, for fishing and whaling were important industries; and in many places, because of the mountains and fiords, the sea was the only channel of communication with the outside world. Commerce was looked on as honorable; it was no shame for these fierce fighters also to be traders. And besides the Vikings at sea there were peaceful merchants who bought or bartered. They sometimes accompanied or followed close behind the raiders, but they themselves were not Vikings. (*Viking* is a word derived from the old Norse. *Vikingr* was a camp used during a raid. A *vik* was a creek or an inlet, the place favored as a starting point of many raids. *Viking* came to mean an expedition of piracy or plunder, or a person who took part in such an expedition.)

Viking raids began as sporadic forays in the late 700s, and were carried out on a larger scale in the early 800s. Once the Scandanavians began, they undertook such raids with well-organized and well-equipped fleets. They went out, as Adam of Bremen wrote, to "wander over the whole world and by their piratical expeditions bring home the greater part of the wealth of the countries." But, they were traders as well, as shown when the Danes made peace with Lugwig the German in 873 "in order. . .that merchants of each kingdom might buy and sell peacefully." As did Cilician, Vandal and earlier pirates, the Norse often sold their booty in the very place it was taken. At Nantes the Northmen once agreed to evacuate on a certain day if their market was not molested before that time.

When they raided, they used their spears, swords, and battle-axes without mercy. One of their effective weapons was the bow and arrow, an instrument not usually thought to be associated with the Norse. In their coats of mail, or their simple jerkins and cloaks, carrying shields made of thin wooden boards, they went by sea to some quiet inlet or up a broad river. Then they took the enemy by surprise. The scouts and fire raisers went ahead, the foragers followed to collect the booty. As the flames spread from hut to house, to the church, and the peasants fled terrified in every direction, the Northmen systematically stripped the settlement, and rounded up captives to be used at home or sold as slaves.

Such raids were individual undertakings; only much later—during the late 10th and early 11th centuries—did they take on the appearance of national endeavors. At first each raid was wholly an under-

The sudden appearance of Viking fleets such as this filled coastal settlements with fear.

taking of a few men banded together for strength. They hit with suddenness and surprise. Once they began a raid they made as much noise as possible to cause confusion and fright. Many peacefully sleeping people awoke with a start to witness scene after scene of nightmare brutality. This was part of the life of the times. If it were not the Norse it could have been the raiders from the neighboring district.

In the beginning, attacks took place only during the warm months when navigation was best. The Anglo-Saxon Chronicle (a record of the deeds of the king and the happenings in Anglo-Saxon territory) tells us that "three ships of Northmen" came and raided in the late 780s. (The Chronicle is without year or date, so the year varies with the whim of the modern writer, usually being set a 787.) The raiders landed near Dorchester, Wessex, and killed one of King Beorthric's officals. "These were the first ships of the Danish men which sought the land of the English nation." (The Britains of the day almost always called any Northman a Dane.) The raiders were probably Norwegians, for many of the versions of this particular

Chronicle say they came from "Herethaland," the west Norwegian district of Hörthland.

These summer raids were sometimes hard to distinquish from ordinary trading voyages. The Swedish people who went viking, for example, entered Russia in independent groups of small armed bands. They warred with the natives as well as with each other; but they traded as much as they raided. These Norsemen, called *Rus* (the word meant rowers, for they came as rowers in their ships) took slaves and furs south through the desolate regions of Russia, into the Black Sea, and even to Constantinople.

Later in history many of these Swedish fighters, as well as Danes and Norwegians, were employed as an elite group of warriors by the Byzantine emperors. They were called Varangians, a term meaning Norsemen or Northmen, and were especially admired because they often proved a bulwark to the unsteady throne. The first Varangians to serve the empire were those who had been captured on a pirate raid in 860. They had come out of Russia to the Black Sea, then into the Bosporus. Here 200 of their vessels were trapped when the Byzantine Mediterranean fleet sailed in from the west and the Black Sea fleet sailed in from the east at the same time. Some of the captured Norsemen became Christians and began their service in Byzantium.

Some Swedish trading expedition were completely peaceful, with traders going under warrior protection, and this was not unusual. Many people of wealth or importance traveled with their own body-guards, or small personal armies, sometimes even in civilized countries, into the 1800s. A peaceful group of Russ traders is recorded in a Frankish annal in 839 accompanying a Byzantine embassy to the Carolingian emperor.

The Swedish Vikings traveled from the Baltic to the Black Sea using the rivers of the region as roadways, and they came eventually to control these rivers. In order to maintain this control they built stockaded trading posts from which they sent out numerous pirate fleets. These outposts developed into rich trade centers, such as Kiev. From Kiev and other trading centers they attacked the ports of the Black Sea, and even Constantinople. Many of these Swedish Vikings settled in Russia, and were able to control much of the commerce in Oriental goods that entered Russia and the Baltic. This led to the growth of a lively merchant class in the Russian settlements as well as in Sweden. Just how vast was this trade is only now being discovered as a result of archeological finds in Sweden. Recently excavated warehouses of the period, with trade goods still in them, indicate that peaceful and well-organized trade was much greater than previously had been suspected. To bring law and order to the region, the Slavs asked the Norse to rule, and the Norse rulers gradually were absorbed into the native groups and coverted to Christianity during the 10th and 11th centuries. Viking raids in the east then ended.

Viking raids were not common in the Mediterranean or on the Spanish peninsula, but they did occur. A fleet of forty-four Norse ships attacked Lisbon in 844. Joined by twenty-six other Viking vessels, this fleet went on to sack Seville, then entered the Mediterranean and raided as far as Necour on North Africa. The most serious attempt of the Norse to establish themselves in the south took place in 858 when a group of Northmen settled on the island of Camaria for two winters. They raided towns on the Mediterranean coast, including Luni and Pisa. These two incidents seem to be the limit of activity of the Norse in the inland sea until 944 when a Norse fleet again appeared off the coasts of Spain and plundered at Cadiz, Seville, and other cities. They returned in 966, but their fleet was beaten off by Spanish Moslems. Ten years later when they came to attack Andulusia once again they faced a powerful Moslem fleet and were easily defeated. The Norse were ineffectual in the Mediterranean. They could not establish themselves here for any long period. The Moslem fleets were too strong and numerous and Moslem seamen—themselves mainly pirates—controlled most of the western Mediterranean.

Perhaps the most effective raids carried out by the Vikings took place in the region that now forms France, Germany, and the Netherlands. Here the Northmen (mostly Danes), using the sea and rivers as highways, encountered little resistance. They seldom left the water. Had they gone overland for any great distance they would have had to engage in serious combat with armed horsemen at many points. Their pirate ventures began as quick raids called *stradhögg*. Slaves were taken, booty gathered, and cattle slaughtered and roasted.

They often raided monasteries, for there the richest booty was to be found—gold and silver. The church in Rome would have liked its

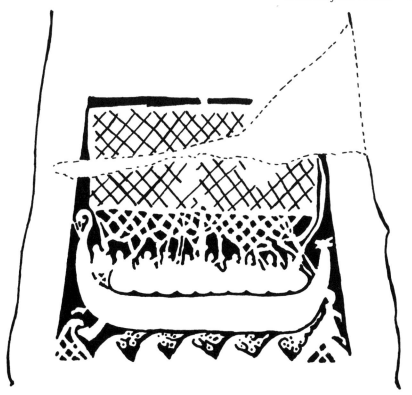

Carving from Gotland, Sweden, showing Norse vessel of the 9th century.

places of worship and its cloisters to be considered sacred, but their wealth often incited even Christian rulers to raid them. Monasteries, and episcopal residences, which were as richly decorated as those of any lord's, were often stripped. The threat of excommunication did not hold the same dread for people during these restless times as it often did in later, more settled times. Although church chronicles would make it seem that the acts of the Norse were exceptional when they plundered religious places, they were not. At this period the sanctity of church property depended on the power of the church to protect itself and on the whim of the ruler on whose land church property was situated. Even the papal residences in Rome were plundered by Christian rulers. It was not uncommon for a Pope to mount his charger and take to the field to rout his enemies.

The Norse raids in Frankish lands were perhaps the most devastating because these lands, unlike the British Isles and Russia, were well settled, relatively civilized, and economically advanced. During long years of strong rule from the time of Clovis (the leader of the Salic Franks who defeated the Roman governor of northern Gaul in 486), to Ludwig the Pious (814–840), the Frankish kingdom had prospered. The serious Norse raids began just as strong central power in these Frankish lands was disintergrating.

In addition to attacking the coastal regions, the Northmen rowed up the rivers from the Elbe to the Garonne. Antwerp was plundered and burned in 836. Paris was plundered a number of times during the 800s. Such inland cities as Tours on the Loire were sacked. The later Carolingians often gave the Northmen money when they appeared, as a bribe for the promise not to attack. Early in the tenth century, when once again they were about to ravish Paris, Charles III (893–923) ceded part of the coast to them, from the edge of Brittany to the Somme.

They had spent many winters in the land, camping, to plunder again when the weather turned fair. Now they had a permanent settlment of their own, and an important one, for it was on the lower course of the Seine, opposite Britain. They measured off the land and divided it among those willing to settle. Thus they created Normandy, a section of Europe that was to have great influence later with the Norman invasion of England, and the Norman conquest of southern Italy, Sicily, Malta, and parts of Greece. Norman fighting forces greatly aided other Europeans in the Crusades to the Holy Land. It was not long after their settlement in Normandy that such Normans as William Longsword (936) occupied high positions in the councils of the Carolingian kings. A short time later, in the 980s, the dukes of Normandy surpassed the king himself in military power.

The Norse made their first tentative stab at the British Isles at the Anglo-Saxon state of Wessex in the late 700's, as we have seen. In 789 they came a second time, and by 793–4 they were plundering many settlements on the island, in the north as well as the south. "Never before," wrote a churchman, "has such terror appeared in Britain as we have now suffered from a pagan race, nor was it thought that such an inroad from the sea could be made." Considering the history of those islands his statement is surprising. The people there were still not wholly Christian then, and were occupied with their own wars. The Norse came at a time when there was widespread disorganization in the British Isles.

In Chapter 5 a brief summary was given of how the rule of Rome came to an end in Britain, and the Saxons, Jutes, and Angles—among the rudest and least civilized of the Gothic peoples—invaded Britain and settled there in the fifth century. They pushed the native Celtic inhabitants into small pockets of land (Cornwall and Wales), and even forced them off the island to regions as far away as Brittany. The Angles and Saxons had much in common, but after their settlement they did not join forces but were continually warring, making isolated Britain a barbaric haunt. The people of Wessex had not progressed far from their rude beginnings. Their conversion to Christianity began shortly before the 600s, and this did have a cohesive and civilizing influence.

Beginning with Ecgberht (823–837) the West Saxon kings, after centuries of warfare, had gained a hold over most of the southern part of the island with overlordships in Mercia, Wales, and other regions. Just then swarms of Norse raiders appeared and began the systematic harassment of the land. They burned and killed and plundered with increasing intensity. In 865 the Saxon king Aethelwulf gave them a money bribe (Danegold, or *Danegeld*) for the first time to restrain their activities.

The payment of this ransom was in keeping with a very old tradition that seems alien to many modern minds. It has within recent years been called "a cowardly act" and "a blot on English history," but it was a practical measure and was the manner in which rulers and cities had dealt with piratical raiders from earliest times. It not only did the job, but saved trouble, lives, and property. It allowed the people in the southern part of this island to survive; there seemed nothing cowardly about that.

The history of *Danegeld* is in itself interesting, and a good example of how such payments were dealt with by the victims of piracy. The payment did not come from the ruler as a personal fee, but was raised as a special tax. The amount of gold and silver paid was staggering; it would be useless to try to convert the sum into present day money since the economic system of the times was so different from our own; but that it most often caused great hardships for the people of the country where it was raised indicates that the amounts were very large indeed.

After its first payment in 865, Danegold was given to the Norse in Britain every few years on an escalating basis. Thousands of pieces of gold and silver were paid in 991, and then twice as much in 994, and nearly double that amount again in 1002, the year of the Massacre of all Danes in England (November 13, 1002, called Danish Vespers) by order of king Ethelred. In 1007 nearly four times as much *Danegeld* as had been paid in 991 was given the Norse.

Ravages by the Northmen were severe in Britain in the early 1000s, and raiding went on until Cnut (Canute), a Dane, became king of England in 1016. The *Danegeld* continued to be collected for a long time afterward, although it was not paid to marauding Northmen. Thomas Becket's opposition to its collection when he became Archbishop of Canterbury was one of the bitter disagreements between Henry II and Becket, disagreements which led eventually to the murder of the archbishop. The tax was finally abolished during Henry's reign (1154–1189).

In 867 a Norse leader, Healfdene, seized York, and after that the raiders settled in Northumbria. They still raided fiercely in East Anglia (beginning in 866), Mercia (beginning in 868) and finally in 878 they ravaged Wessex itself. They were so successful that they forced the king, Alfred the Great, to take refuge with what remained of his hounded forces. Alfred was a vigorous warrior on land and sea, as well as a great politician and administrator. It is said that he personally designed ships that were an improvement on the Viking vessels and that he was responsible for defeating a Viking fleet at sea. There is no firm evidence from this era to substantiate these claims, and no one has any idea what improvements he made on Viking ships. Some writers have "guessed" the improvement was made at the sides of the vessels, others that it had something to do with decking the ships; but these "guesses" were made centuries after the king was dead.

In 879 Alfred came to terms with the Norse. A treaty was signed with Guthorm, the Viking leader, at Wedmore. Guthorm was given the eastern part of the island (Britain) for settlement. From then to the Norman conquest (1066) was an unstable time, with alternating war, trade, and fusion among the settled raiders and the various island peoples.

People throughout Europe were praying, "From the fury of the Northmen, deliver us, O God." Yet the Scandinavians' life at home was, in some ways, not so primitive as it was among some of their neighbors. The Norse had a strong feeling for law. They had contact with the civilized East. (Harold Hardrada, who became King of Norway, had been a commander among the Varangians; he served on the Danube, in the Aegean, and in Sicily before coming to the throne.) The Norse were skilled administrators, and this made them natural leaders in the lands where they settled. At home there were wealthy merchants, prosperous farmers, lawgivers, poets, and many others who peacefully went about their daily business.

The Norse went from simple pirate attacks to longer expeditions and then to colonization. Often they came to rule the regions where they settled. They settled and developed Iceland in 874, and Greenland about a hundred years later. They discovered North America and briefly settled there. They were the first European people to travel extensively and for great distances on the open oceans of the West. The ships and maritime techniques used by the Norse helped in the later migrations of European peoples, and in the development of long oceanic routes.

The ships the Norse used were an important feature of their success as pirates. They have a surprising history that is still somewhat of a mystery. For centuries the Scandinavians used vessels without sail. Tacitus, the Roman historian (ca. 57–117 A.D.) described these vessels as being different in shape from Roman craft. He wrote that "having a prow at each end, they are always ready for running on to the beach. They are not worked by sails, nor are the oars fastened to the sides in regular order, but left loose as [oars are on vessels] in some rivers, so that they can be shifted here and there as circumstances may require."

It is something of a wonder that in pre-Viking days the Norse ships were powered solely by oars. Pictorial evidence indicates that sails and rowlocks and rowing holes were introduced about the time the Norwegians began to sail in the North Sea to the islands off Scotland and Ireland. They settled in Ireland as early as 830 at

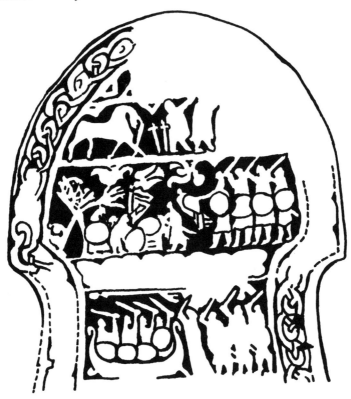

Carved stone from Gotland, Sweden, showing Norse during an attack from the sea.

Armagh. Olaf the White of Norway founded Dublin which lasted as a Norse settlement until 1014. Describing the ships used by the Veneti, who were neighbors of the Scandanavians in the North, Julius Caesar reported that their vessels had sails and were accustomed to sail to Britain. He described the sails of the Veneti as being made of raw hides and thinly-dressed skins. When the Norse made their appearance in the North on the sea, this is what their sails also were made of.

On their piratical voyages the Norse probably most often used cargo vessels, *knorrs,* and not their famous warships or "long ships." A *knorr* was capable of carrying up to 150 men. There were many other Scandanavian vessels in use at the time, and some, no doubt, were taken on pirate expeditions, including the *hafskip,* a sea-going merchant vessel, as well as various rowed vessels.

If the sagas of the North are to be believed, the famous Norse long ship, or Dragon Ship (drekkar), did not come into existence until the very end of the 900s. In the story of King Olaf Tryggvason there is the description of the first one built. By the time this vessel had been built the Norse had been raiding for over two centuries. Such long ships were rowed by from forty to eighty men. Cnut, who was no doubt one of the greatest Norse leaders of the early 1000s, had a ship with a hundred and twenty rowers, but this seems to have been an expection.

The Norse, it must be remembered, were not only raiders on land, but were fierce pirates at sea. Like the Carthaginians in the Mediterranean, the Norse considered all foreign vessels enemy shipping. And many times Norse raiding fleets came upon fellow Norse raiders with whom they fought brutal sea battles. One fleet or flotilla would come to grips with another in neat formation, like cavalry, with each leader's vessel surrounded by his ships and warriors, much as a charging nobleman on land would charge surrounded by his

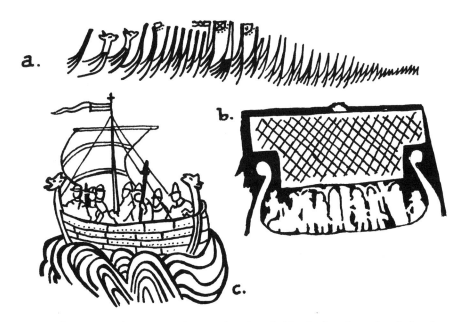

Prows of Norse vessels. *a.* Norwegian woodcarving of ships in fleet formation during the 1200s shows a variety of prows; *b.* Swedish 9th-century vessel with curled prow; *c.* Danish vessel with animal head at the prow and stern, shown in a fresco painted in the 1300s.

knights. The enemy tried to break up the opponant's formation with the aim of sinking or capturing the leader's vessel. Arrows, spears, rocks, barrels, oars, and even ashes from spent fires, and slacked lime were used as missiles. Ramming was attempted, for sinking the enemy was considered the best way to win on the sea. But, if this was accomplished the booty would be lost, so when capture was the aim—not victory, as in war—the Norse preferred to board.

The ships used by the Norse on their pirate raids strongly influenced the maritime history of western Europe. Most of the merchant vessels of the north were built along the same lines as Viking craft during the years following the Vikings' piratical activity. Built in the German towns of Cologne, Hamburg, and Lubeck (all part of the Hanseatic League that, in later years, developed extensive long-distance openwater commerce), the vessels were adoptations of the earlier Scandanavian craft. The ships used by the Normans, as would be expected, were built like Norse ships at the time of the Norman invasion of England. As late as the 1400s in drawings of London the

English coastal vessel of 1170–1185.

smaller ships at the docks often appear very similar to earlier Norse coastal vessels.

The difference between the later merchant ships, usually referred to as "Hansa cogs" or simply as "cogs," and the Norse vessels was that the later craft were carvel-built, that is the planks at the side were placed one a-top the other, resulting in a smooth surface, while the Norse vessels had been clinker-built, with the planks overlapping as in a clapboard house. In addition, the Norse ships were simply large open vessels using sail, although they had been designed also to be propelled by oars; the ships that followed were double-ended but decked, and they mainly employed sails. Slowly the stern of northern ships became rounded, and the steering oar, or "steer-board," was abandoned. Taking its place was a stern rudder strongly hinged to a solid sternpost. The stern rudder was probably first used in northern Europe in the late 1100s. (Stern rudders can be seen in temple carvings from as early as A.D. 800 in India.)

Cogs were made into warships by building platforms, called castles, at each end. When these vessels were used in war or piracy (in wartime mainly as troop ships), the castles served as fighting stations for archers and missile throwers; when they were returned to commercial use the platforms were removed. Gradually such castles came to be built as permanent platforms on the ship just beyond the stempost and in front of the sternpost. When the castles were built directly into the bow and the stern as an integral part of the ship's hull it produced a new vessel type, the carrack.

With the final settlement of the Northmen a large area of the North was economically linked, including present-day Norway, Denmark, Ireland, Sweden, England, Northern France, and other sections of Europe. Normans were trading as far down the Atlantic as the Ivory and Gold Coasts of Africa; English vessels were fishing off Iceland; Danes were sailing on peaceful trading missions to Lisbon; and all these groups traded with each other. European trade was extended by the roving Norse in the Middle Ages as it had been by the Italian cities of the south.

With commerce on the open oceans stimulated, trade centers grew. They were built in strong defensible locations since Norse and other pirates still sailed the seas. Because the Norse proved so effective as pirates and raiders, shore defenses in the areas they attacked

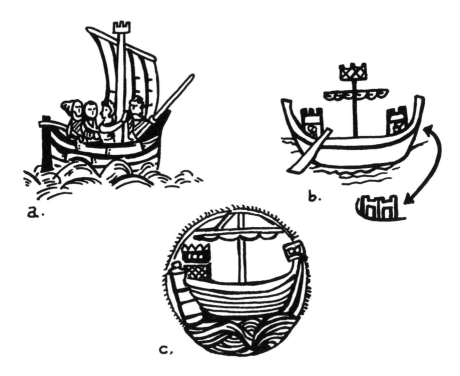

Vessels of the 1200s were converted to warships by adding temporary castles. *a.* German vessel of mid-1200s has hinged rudder and no castles; *b.* seal of the town of Dunwhich used during the 1200s shows steering oar and castles built in the prow and stern of a ship; *c.* seal of the town of Ipswich in the 1200s shows the steering oar and castles built in a vessel.

were increased. There was a general erection of castles after their rempaging invasion of 862 in Frankish lands. The circulation of the silver and gold taken from the nobility and the church stimulated commerce. This circulation of money came at a time when new silver mines were opened in Alsace (800s), and in the Black Forest and Harz Mountains (900s), and this helped to some degree to check the tendency of precious metals to flow toward the East. Norse ships, and later Hanseatic business methods, were the instruments used in the new oceanic maritime adventures. Soon the traditions of the North and South would join, introducing the age of discovery and expansion, which in turn introduced new piratical activities that gave the word piracy a new meaning.

Wrecks and Wrecking

During the late Middle Ages ships still mainly traveled from "view to view." Staying close to the coast often led to grounding on rocks and reefs not known to the navigator.

Laws that could be traced back to ancient Rhodes concerning wrecks stipulated that a wreck belonged to the noble on whose coast the ship foundered. Owners, however, had three months to claim the wreck if there were survivors aboard. Then, by custom, a portion of the ship's cargo was given to the local lord for the time and trouble involved in the transaction.

Purposely wrecking ships was one form of piracy. The practice of luring a ship into shallow or rocky waters by the use of false beacons was common along certain coasts. Penalties for wrecking varied from country to country. If it were proven that human life had been taken during a wrecking operation, the wrecker might be stoned to death; in some countries, England among them, the wrecker was chained to a post in his house and the house set afire.

New wrecking laws were introduced during the thirteenth and fourteenth centuries when maritime law codes were adopted in the north and among the emerging Italian port cities. Underlying these wrecking laws was the priciple that if any person or animal were alive when the wreck was found, the ship was not to be considered abandoned; therefore, it was not open to claim by anyone but the proper shareholders. Previously in the north a local lord claimed any wreck discovered in his territory. Any merchandise on a wrecked vessel became his, and surviving passengers and crewmen were his prisoners, sometimes for many years. These prisoners were used as hostages in exchange for prisoners held by the ruler of the country from which the passengers and crew came. Sometimes they were sold as slaves, and sometimes they were ransomed. The new laws concerning wrecks changed these practices. In regions where wrecking was a tradition, however, the change was hardly for the better, for the new laws led to the death of innocent voyagers who survived a shipwreck only to be killed by wreckers so that the vessel could be claimed as an abandoned one.

8. Modern Privateering

From the 1300s to the 1500s commerce in the waters around Europe began more and more to fall into two distinct categories: local or coastal, and oceanic or international. Piracy followed commerce, and now, encouraged by various rulers, pirate fleets often augmented or took the place of national navies. The story of piracy along the English and French coasts bordering the channel that divided these territories is the story of the beginning of a new age of piracy—the age of modern privateering. Control of this channel became vitally important to the English after the loss of Normandy and other continental territories. The danger of invasion was very real; the island had been successfully invaded many times before.

Looking at the history of this area, we see that the numerous bitter battles fought on land and at sea between England and France during the 13th and 14th centuries were fought mainly because the rulers of England were actually Norman. Henry II (1133–1189) and Richard I (1157–1199) should more properly be called French lords rather than Englishmen, for that was how they saw themselves. The kingdom of England was small compared to their vast holdings in France. John Lackland, who reigned from 1199 to 1216, and who signed the Magna Charta, was the first "truly" English king of the House of Anjou (Plantagenet), for his kingdom was confined mainly to the English section of the British Isles.

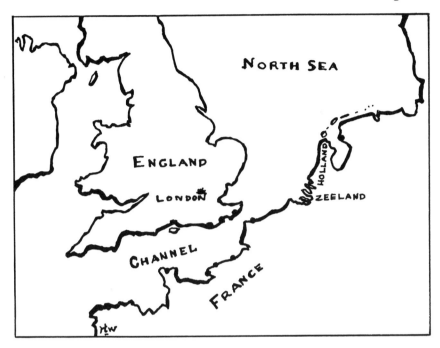

The Channel between England and France.

Piracy became part of this tapestry of war because England was then not a maritime power. It was not to be truly oceanic-minded until Stuart rule in the early 1600s (see page 146). Almost all of the country's shipping was confined to fishing, not transport; almost all the goods entering or leaving the land went in foreign vessels, primarily under the control of the Hanseatic League (see Appendix A). Still, the channel carried a great deal of commerce in fish, wool, and wine, and this commerce was hard hit when Philip II of France took Normandy (1203–1204) from King John (which is how the name Lackland arose). The pirate war that was to shape the future of piracy began now as a series of retaliatory measures against the French for the "lost provinces" of the Norman kings of England.

Pirates were employed by both rulers. One of the first was Eustace the Monk, backed by King John. Eustace, a monk who had left the clergy when he killed a man in a duel, took service with the Count of Boulogne, but he proved a troublemaker and had to flee the Continent. He offered his services to King John and was put in

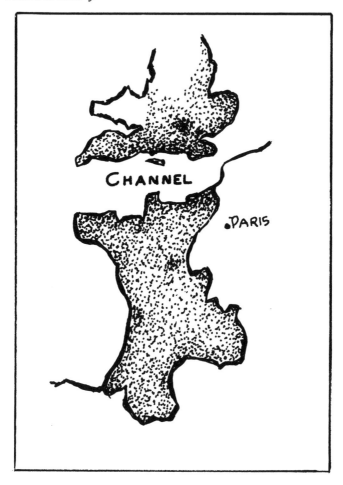

Lands of the Plantagenet king Henry II (1154–1189) in France and England.

charge of a small fleet. Under his leadership, the ships successfully raided among the islands of the Channel and along the French coast. Eustace sailed on many a piratical voyage for the English, and was much feared by the French. Philip II could not grarantee safe passage to England for any ship, not even that of the Papal Legate to whom he wrote, "...if you fall into the hands of Eustace the Monk...do not put the blame on us."

In 1212 Eustace changed sides in favor of Philip II, who gladly outfitted him with ships. He then went off to raid along the coasts and amid the islands of the Channel against English ports and against

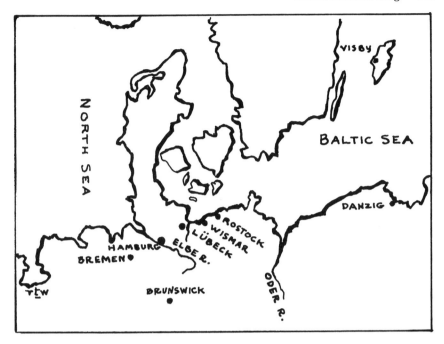

Important cities of the Hanseatic League.

ships transporting English goods. His piratical acts were decribed as the bloodiest of the time. The tales about him and his exploits, however, seem often to be exaggerated, as when one chronicler describes Eustace's last battle; such enormous amounts of blood from dying men flowed into the sea, it was said, that it coagulated into great scarlet globs as large as bolts of cloth.

A sea battle during the 1300s.

Pirate raiding continued unabated during the 1200s. Some of the pirates were issued licenses by the king, thus making "privateers" of the "pirates." In 1243 Henry III granted such licenses to Adam Robernolt and William le Sauvage "to annoy our enemies at sea and by land wheresoever they are able, so that they share with us half of all their gain." (Similar licenses were issued by church officials and rulers in the Mediterranean against Moslem shipping.) Such arrangements were of ancient origin. They did not originate, as is often believed, in the reign (1272-1307) of Edward I, although formal letters of marque were issued by Edward's lieutenant in Gascony to Bernard d'Ongressill after d'Ongressill's ship had been captured at sea. This enabled him legally to return to sea and capture a vessel, or vessels, approximately equal to the value of his lost ship. His piratical action then would have the approval of his government, and in England it would be considered legal privateering, not piracy.

Enabling a sea-going trader to go "on the plundering account" instead of the ordinary "business account," letters of marque were based on merchant laws used by the medieval guilds. The laws allowed a merchant to seize goods of another trader if payment had not been made on a previous purchase. Sea and land uses of the term *marque* were corrupted, for the medieval Latin word *marcare,* used in such laws, simply meant to seize as a pledge. *(Privateer,* meaning a private man-of-war, or the commander of such a vessel, came into use in the 1600s.) The law logically carried over to the sea, for part of its provision allowed the seizure or detention of vessels in port if the default of payment took place in a port city. Maritime letters of marque gave the injured party repayment for the amount defaulted plus damages.

Such letters were supposed to be issued to *authorized officials* who then collected the debt, and not to the injured party. But a maritime venture was risky; it involved crews and parties not involved in the default. Besides if the seizure of a ship took place at sea—which it almost always did as the years passed—a battle invariably ensued. So, in order to protect the life of the authorized offical, maritime letters of marque were issued to the merchant whose shipping had been pirated. That was the theory. In fact, as time passed they were almost soley issued to men whose fighting ability had been proven at sea, and such men were not scrupulous about the ships they attacked. Often enemy and friend were both subject to capture on the sea.

The difficulty of controlling an individual who was issued such a letter of reprisal is at once obvious. What was to stop a privateer from plundering an amount far greater than his estimated loss plus damage? And, once begun, who was to issue a counter order demanding an account and punishment if a privateer turned to outright piracy? Who would go against the king and his officers when the king himself was collecting part of the profits from privateering?

Men fought, pleaded, and intrigued to get letters of marque, for they could be the means of gaining a fortune. Such letters continued to be prized for generations, but governments issuing them found that they often impeded war efforts. Thus, during the American War of Independence when congress issued letters of marque, they hindered development of the Continental Navy, for they opened up a field of activity much more lucrative than service on Continental frigates and armed vessels. (See Appendix F.)

An English and French encounter in the Channel, 1217. The roundish object at the end of the arrow on the left is what the French called a "pot de feu," or jar of fire. It was an incendiary grenade filled with pitch and powder, and was used like a modern "Molotov cocktail." The English called this a "fire pot." Captain John Smith mentioned large fire pots filled with pitch, powder, and stones that "in a crowd of people will make incredible laughter."

French vessel of the early 1200s. The artist shows the castles as houses. The fort built toward the stern, with chimney and smoke, was the invention of an imaginative mind. The single mast and square sail were common on ships of the North at the time.

Piracy and privateering occurred more and more in the Channel during Edward's reign. Such piracy was sometimes backed with letters of marque, but more often the incidents were independent and illegal. Letters of marque were a favor conferred by the king. They were not easy to come by without some influence at court.

With the encouragement of Edward I, English ships increasingly attacked French ships, and the French, of course, retaliated. In 1293 pirate attacks by groups on both sides of the Channel led to a large-scale engagement. "English" ships (which were actually Irish, Dutch, Gascon, and English) engaged "French" ships (which were actually Norman, Breton, and Flemish). The "English" were victorious; but instead of pleasing him, the victory alarmed Edward who was busily engaged in a war with the Scots. He did not want war with the French at the same time. He demanded an explanation from the barons of the Cinque Ports (an association of towns in southeastern England important in defending the coast), who were the chief instigators of the battle. They wrote a lengthy protest of innocence, telling of a series of hostile French actions and outrages. It stated that:

> On the Friday before Pentecoat [April 14, 1293] they came in sight with two hundred ships, crammed with armed men in bow and stern, and with banner of red cendal flying, each of two ells in width and thirty in length,[1] which are called "bucans," [see Appendix B] and by the English "streamers," and these signify amongst all men of the sea death without quarter and mortal war. In this way the Normans came down upon your people and feloniously attacked them contrary to the peace. Your people defended themselves and God by His grace gave them victory.

The French King, Philip IV (1268–1314) was so outraged that he summoned the English king to court, for Philip was Edward's overlord in connection with the continental possessions of Gascony and Guienne. Edward did not appear, but he sent his brother. Philip, however, was not satisfied, and again he demanded Edward's presence. When Edward—at war with the Welsh now—did not appear after a third summons Philip, in 1294, declared the English king's lands in France forfeited. War followed between Philip and Edward.

What had been acts of piracy were now acts of war and, as a monk of the day expressed it, "There was no law imposed upon the sailors, but whatever any one could carry off, that he called his own"—a good description of circumstances at sea even as they had been before the war began.

Acts of piracy went on during the 1300s with increasing frequency. Vessels were sent with wool from England under escort to Antwerp. They were often attacked; some were cut out by Gallic pirates while at sea, and others attacked at anchor. English pirates, such as John Lambot, indulged so much in the torturing of captives and were so numerous that they were even outlawed in England. French piratical activity was on a similar level.

Early in the 1300s there were 117 reported attacks on shipping in one year in English waters, ranging from assault on the wool fleet to the capturing of a Genoese vessel at anchor off the English coast. During the reign (1307–1321) of Edward II, the number of pirates on the waters of the Channel was given as approximately 7,000. No matter how approximate such estimates are, they give a general picture of the times. Travel by sea must have been dangerous, indeed.

---

[1] One ell, an old measure of length, is 45 inches.

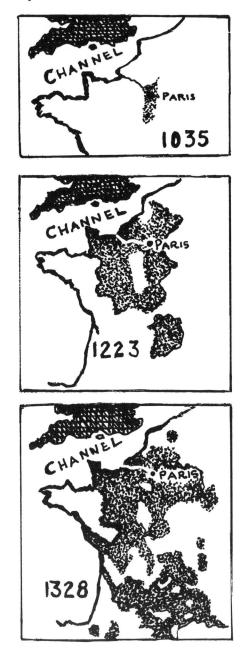

The growth of France. Much of the land previously had been under the control of English kings. The pirate war between England and France (13th and 14th centuries) was fueled by the hope of regaining these "lost provinces."

Torture was common in the North as well as in the Mediterranean. Here a captive is dismembered by four vessels that sail off in different directions.

Considering that neither England nor the French territories were maritime powers, and that England, especially, was thinly populated, the number of pirates operating on this one small patch of water, the Channel, seems surprisingly large.

These were the days when a king could order his knights to put his ship alongside the enemy so that he could "have a tilt with him." The method of fighting used by pirate and king was still "in-fighting," that is boarding. "Off-fighting," or fighting at a distance, did not come into existence until the use of cannon became an important factor in naval engagements. Until cannon became common, pirates used various weapons. A new and efficient one was the Welsh long-bow adapted by the English under the encouragement of Edward I. The ships' castles were used as platforms for the archers. Still, it was in hand-to-hand fighting that the encounter at sea was won or lost.

During battle at sea grappling was common, with the pirates or warriors throwing grappling hooks, then drawing the attacked vessel to the side of their vessel in order to board. At times snares, or nets, were used, thrown over the defenders of a vessel as nets are used to ensnare birds. Ramming was sometimes attempted by both pirate or fighter, but with pirates it was used more to disable than to sink. Ramming was not nearly so much a part of a sea battle in the North as it was in the Mediterranean, although it was sometimes attempted. Bulky sailing vessels were used in the open waters of the North during this period, and they were not easily maneuverable. In the Mediterranean, galleys were the favored fighting craft into the 16th century, and ramming by a swift, easily maneuverable oared galley was an effective tactic, often favored, especially against smaller craft.

When the melee was over usually all on board the captured vessel were trussed up by the pirates and thrown into the sea. (It is difficult to understand why the wounded were often strangled before being thrown over the side, but it is said to have been the practice with Channel pirates of the time.) Torture was common, carried out on fellow countrymen as well as foreigners. Priests and clerics, who at the time had such great power on land and many special priveleges above the ordinary citizen, were flogged and subject to special indignities. The captured vessel was rifled for valuables, then towed to port where the cargo was sold. The captured ship then might become part of the pirate fleet or it might be sold, for the vessel itself was, perhaps, the most valuable and important single piece of plunder. Only occasionally would jewels, gold, or special cargo such as pepper surpass the value of the ship.

At this time, and afterward, a great deal of piracy on the sea was conducted by merchant associations, leagues, and companies conducting transport business with government charters. (The sea has been, and is today, the best and cheapest highway for the exchange of goods.) The piracy indulged in by such merchant groups was part of the legacy of maritime conduct from the ancient world where the right to hinder economic rivals at sea was never questioned. Whether such acts of piracy might more appropriately be called a form of privateering depends more on their historical context than on maritime ethics. The ancient Greeks and Carthaginians had no qualms about such piracy being proper conduct. Merchants of the Middle Ages felt much the same way.

Letters of marque often led from reprisal to reprisal, which led to further attacks at sea between seamen and merchants of two hostile nations. After the 1400s piracy became less important then privateering. Thus, the historic record of piracy in the Atlantic is in large part the story of privateering and of officially encouraged piracy. Privateering spread from the Channel to the islands of the Atlantic, such as the Azores, then to the Caribbean and the waters off the coast of the Americas. Even when a vessel was not operated under a letter of marque much of this piracy was privateering, as in the case of English and French piracy in the West Indies during the 1500s against the Spanish—it had government approval and encouragement, although at times not overtly so. (See page 144.)

Pirates from the Netherlands and France swarmed the Channel during the later part of the 1500s. They pirated mostly Spanish ships and sold them in English ports. These pirates were not the famous "Sea Beggers." The true Sea Beggers had their beginnings in the revolt of the lesser nobility of the Netherlands in 1566. This revolt was against the Spanish regent of the country, Margaret of Parma, Philip II of Spain's Netherlands-born half sister. On April 3, 1566 the lesser nobility presented her with a bill of indictment against her government. They called themselves "Leaguers." The regent accepted the indictment, but she was furious, and worried about loosing control of the country. On leaving the assembly one of her counselors, Count Berlaymont, said to her, *"Ce n'est qu'un tas de gueux,"*— "They're nothing but a bunch of beggers."

The leaders of the minor nobility held a banquet that evening, and one among them, Count Brederode, having heard about Berlaymont's comment, produced a pouch and wooden bowl used by beggers, and shouted: *"Vivent les Gueux!"* *Gueux,* or Beggers, became the name of the party taking part in this minor revolt which eventually led to war between the people of the Low Countries and the Spanish government.

In March of 1567 the royalists favoring Spanish rule regained control of the country. The Beggers party broke up, and some became *Gueux de Mer,* or Sea Beggers. Operating as a group, they raided Spanish shipping. This was simple piracy; but the Prince of Orange who came over to the rebel side had the right to issue letters of marque by virtue of his sovereign powers. Such letters, issued to captains of ships which flew his flag, made the Beggers legal privateers.

The Prince of Orange laid down strict standards for their behavior. Hostile acts were to be conducted only against the new regent's regime, that is, the government of the Duke of Alva in the Netherlands. Christian piety was to be observed by the crews, and only seaman who could prove a "good character" were allowed to take part in the war at sea.

At first the Sea Begger fleet consisted of only twenty-five ships. They had no base from which to operate so they landed and gathered supplies wherever they could. The spring of 1572 found a small squadron of these privateers in English waters, recovering from a serious beating at Spanish hands. But Elizabeth I, formerly a friend to the Sea Beggers, now favored the Duke of Alva, for she was beginning to fear Dutch sea power. English officals made it clear to the Beggers that they would no longer be welcome in England. Sailing back to the Low Countries they captured the town of Brill which had been left unprotected by the Spanish. From Brill they went to Flushing; there they led the fishermen of the area in an uprising. Veere-on-Walcheren was the next town the privateers captured, again due to the support of local fishermen. Eventually they incited the whole of the northern section of the Netherlands to revolt, and this was the nucleus of the future Dutch Republic. The Sea Beggers, with their daring deeds at sea and on land, were responsible for the succassful spread of the revolt against Spanish rule.

The main base of the Sea Beggers, once they were again established in the Netherlands, was in Zeeland on a group of islands protected from the mainland by seas and rivers. They operated during the same period that Huguenot pirates, as well as Dutch pirates, were considered the scorge of the Channel; but the Sea Beggers used the profit from the sale of their booty to continue their war for independence.

The vessels the Sea Beggers used were called *fluyts,* or flyboats. They were fast, shallow-draft ships, with relatively flat bottoms. At first they were narrow with sloping sides, but gradually during the next century the flyboats were built with wider decks and took on the appearance of small galleons.

The rebellious Sea Beggers acting as privateers, along with other Dutch pirates, commanded the control of the coastal waters of the Low Countries. This was important because it allowed trade to continue and the rebellion against Spain to be maintained, and eventually to succeed.

9. Barbary Corsairs, 1400-1800

Many citizen of the United States remember the story of incidents when this country, early in its history, paid protection money and ransom to the Barbary States in North Africa. To some, these incidents seem a blemish on American history. Examined objectively, however, and in their own time frame, these events can be seen as part of the pattern of piracy that had existed from ancient times. (See chapter 7 for similar incidents—the payment of Danegold by the Saxons—and a similar reaction.)

The beginning of the story has already been told in previous chapters. Pirates had operated out of the ports of North Africa since the establishment of the Phoenician colony of Carthage; the Vandal pirate fleets of Roman times appeared next, then followed the Arab-Berber fleets of the early Moslem caliphates. The name Barbary itself is derived from the early Arab period; in Arabian the word *Berber* meant the aboriginal people who lived to the west and south of Egypt. The Berber, or Barbary, coast extended from the west of Egypt to the Atlantic Ocean just past the Straits of Gibraltar. Along the coast of the Mediterranean the Moslem Barbary states were Tripoli, Tunis, Algiers, and Morocco.

Over the centuries various Moslem dynasties controlled these states. About 1300 the Ottoman turks settled in Anatolia. The Ottomans were not a special tribe of Turks, but a group of Turkish warriors called *ghazis*. Gradually the power of the *ghazis* spread, and they became supreme in what is present-day Turkey. The Byzantine empire was not strong enough during this period to check their advances and eventually a great Ottoman army captured the city of Constantinople in 1453 (incidently causing the flight of scholars from that city to Italian universities, which gave a new beat to the European Renaissance).

Under Ottoman rule the people of Constantinople experienced many changes. The Moslem religion replaced Christianity, and Turkish replaced Greek as the offical language, although in other Moslem states the language remained Arabic. After the capture of the city the Turkish sultan was in nominal control of the whole Islamic world. He became the caliph of all Moslems, and controlled (indirectly) the Islamic countries of the east and of North Africa.

During the late 1400s Ottoman sea power was used to contain European advances in the Aegean. The Turks did not shut off trade between Europe and the Orient. Instead they profitted by having merchandise from the east pass through Ottoman territory by caravan in order to avoid going by ship through the Red Sea or Persian Gulf. Voyagers on either of these bodies of water faced many hazards. Hundreds of miles of waterless desert flanked the northern half of the Red Sea and a captain could not be sure of supplying his crew with fresh water. Navigation was made dangerous by the coral reefs that ran along the coasts and that in places extended far out to sea. The most important deterrent to trade and travel on these waters, however, were the pirates who used the coral islands of the area as bases. The nomads on both sides of the Red Sea were, because of harsh living-conditions, eager to attack passing ships. There were few good harbors in which to seek safety in case of storm or when fleeing pirates. Similar conditions in the Persian Gulf, with lack of watering places and with pirates based on the many islands, made travel there precarious, also. To avoid such dangers traders commonly sent or took their goods by the overland camel routes.

With the coming of the Turks, Moslem piracy in the Aegean decreased, but their rule did not diminish piracy elsewhere in the Mediterrean. After 1460 Venice was strong enough to discourage much of the Moslem piracy in the Adriatic, but in 1470 the Ottoman rulers built a great fleet of about 300 ships to supress Venetian sea power in the Aegean. On seeing the Ottoman fleet a Venetian galley captain reported that the many masts appeared to be "a forest on the sea." The Turks used this great fleet to capture one of Venice's main bases in Greece, Negroponte.

Such Turkish fleets were not, however, used to patrol the Aegean at this time. After the capture of Negroponte the ships sailed back to the Dardanells and the city of Constantinople, leaving the islands and port cities of the eastern Mediterranean unprotected. This allowed squadrons of European pirates to raid at will, especially those from the Italian cities and states. After many years of such raids by both Moslems and Christians, the Ottoman rulers began to send out regular patrols against the pirates. In order to further control piracy they conquered Rhodes in 1522, expelling the Knights of the Order of St. John, who were responsible for much of the piracy, from the Aegean.

During the first half of the 1500s, however, piracy also increased among the Moslems themselves, especially along the Barbary Coast where it became highly organized. This occured because early in the century the sultan appointed a Greek-born pirate who had risen to be ruler of Algiers, as chief admiral of his fleet. His name was Khair-ad-Din, known to us as Red Beard, or Barbarossa.

Barbarossa's rise to power began in the 1490s in the Aegean where he and his brother, Horuk, were pirates. Horuk appears to have been the leader in their early years. It was he who approached the ruler of Tunis when the brothers had been hounded out of the Aegean by Turkish patrols; he asked to be allowed to use that city as a base while on pirate missions against Spain. Later the ruler of Algiers asked the brothers to assist him in fighting a Spanish fleet. Instead of giving assistance the brothers captured the city and deposed the ruler in 1516. A few years later Horuk was murdered, and Khair-ad-Din became the head of the Algerian state. Under his leadership Moslem naval forces and Moslem pirate fleets were welded into effective fighting units.

In 1534 Khair-ad-Din ravaged southern Italy and other coasts in Europe. In 1538 he led the victorious Turkish fleet in a sea battle against European forces off Greece. The admiral of the Europeans was the Genoese, Andrea Doria, who had himself built a fortune on piracy. It was not Doria's fault that the battle was lost, for Emperor Charles V, the Hapsburg ruler of Spain, the Netherlands, and portions of Germany and Italy, who controlled the European naval squadrons was negotiating with Khair-ad-Din right up to the eve of the battle. He was trying to get Khair-ad-Din to leave the service of the sultan and ally himself with Spanish and Venetian interests, and he did not permit Doria to fight with his full capabilities. For the next thirty years Turkey was largely in control of many Mediterranean sea lanes. When Khair-ad-Din died in 1546, he was followed by leaders he had trained to take his place. One named Torghud, generally known today as the notorious Dragut, attacked and landed on Malta in 1547.

Piracy continued to be a strong tradition along the Barbary coast for basically economic reasons. In the late 1000s nomads destroyed much of the elaborate irrigation system that had been developed in the days of Carthage and Rome. Many of the ancient cities, now found in ruin and surrounded by desert, were in ancient times encircled with verdant fields of grain. The barbary states, Tunis especially, still exported grain, but on a greatly reduced level compared to the days when the area was the bread-basket of Rome. The payment of ransom and tribute to the Barbary rulers, as well as the money paid to them by the corsairs based there for the privilege of using their ports, augumented their income.

European corsairs operated out of Spanish, French, and Italian ports, but their main base was on Malta. Charles V had come into possesion of the island in 1520, shortly afterward he gave it to the Knights of the Order of St. John. When they accepted Malta, the order's name became the Knights of Malta, but they were still commonly referred to as the Knights of St. John. During most of the 1500s the corsairs of Malta were not of great importance in the Mediterranean. With the coming of a grand master named Verdalle, however, they began to grow and become well-organized. When he took charge of the order in 1581, Grand Master Verdalle equipped ships of his own and sent them raiding with his blessings. He strongly urged others in the order to do the same. In 1680 the Knights of Malta drafted rules of conduct for all corsairs operating out of Malta. They had begun issuing a type of pirate's license (called *patente de corso*) in 1605, and they were to go on issuing these licenses until 1798.

The presence of well-organized pirates on the Barbary coast made Malta stategically important to the Europeans. The island is almost exactly in the middle of the Mediterranean at one of its narrowest points, between Sicily and Tripoli. It was difficult for Moslem shipping to pass this point without being detected and attacked, particularly ponderous Moslem convoys. After the establishement of the Knights on Malta, and the development of their corsair fleet, the Barbary pirates were forced to operate mainly in the western Mediterranean and the Atlantic, while Maltese corsairs operated mainly in the eastern Mediterranean.

The sea battle of Lepanto (1571) between the Ottoman Empire and Europeans led by Spain helped to further define this division of the Mediterranean for the next 250 years. From the Turkish point of view the battle was fought to prevent the re-establishment of European power in the eastern Mediterranean. From the European viewpoint, the battle took place to prevent further Ottoman advances in the Adriatic beyond its southern shore. Led by Don Juan of Austria, the half brother of Philip II of Spain, the European forces achieved a victory. Still, shortly afterward, Venice lost most of its bases in the Aegean to Turkey, for Philip II did not allow the European fleet to remain concentrated in the east since he did not wish to see Venice grow too strong.

The battle of Lepanto "drew the line," with the Europeans retaining control from the northern shores of Dalmatia to the Straits of Gibraltar, and the Moslems controlling the coasts of the Mediterranean from Albania to the Atlantic on the southern shores. The battle also caused the European countries to realize that if they were to continue to trade with the Near East and Orient they would have to deal directly with the Ottoman sultan. Thus, Spain signed a peace treaty with the Turks in 1580, and the English and Dutch followed suit shortly after. (The French and Turkish fleets had been in alliance since the days of Khair-ad-Din.)

In the early 1600s two well-organized and active groups of corsairs emerged, one on Malta, the other in ports of the Barbary states. Piracy still occurred in the Aegean and Adriatic and elsewhere, but on a diminished scale. The Ventians hunted pirates, as did the Turks; even the rulers of the Barbary states and the Maltese hunted pirates who were not part of their own corsair fleets. At one time (1735), the Bey of Tunis even sought the help of Malta's religious order to put down piracy in Tunisian waters. It can be said that after Lepanto the general pirate war in the Mediterrean was over, and in its place a restricted war took place. Pirates began to operate in small, efficent fleets.

It is curious that by the 1600s merchant vessels in Mediterranean waters were predominantly sailing vessels, yet the corsairs still often used galleys, as did the navies in southern Europe. Shortly after the battle of Lepanto the use of small carracks, the many-decked merchant vessels that followed the cogs as the favored cargo ships in Europe, increased in the Mediterranean because they had proved better vessels in the Atlantic on the north-south routes, both in surviving storms and in defending themselves against pirates.

Perhaps the corsairs' continued use of galleys was due merely to tradition, perhaps to the fact that galleys were swift and manueverable attack ships. They were especially attractive to corsairs of the Barbary coast, and this is surprising because the main objective of these pirates was to board as quickly as possible and subdue those defending the ships they attacked, and boarding from a galley was awkward. In the mid-1600s a Venetian, Giovanbattista Salvago, wrote, "The Barbary corsairs do not entertain themselves by firing cannon; they seek to board."

The Maltese, on the other hand, although they also frequently used galleys, relied on guns. This made their ships heavier, but it also made the eventual boarding less costly in terms of loss of life. (Corsair galleys were lighter than galleys used in trade because they went to sea unladen with cargo.) Individual cargo vessels that the Maltese corsairs encounted usually surrendered rather than be blown out of the water. The same was true of small European cargo vessels when facing Moslem corsairs. Individual ships generally gave in to the Moslems rather than resist and be killed during the boarding. Yet there are so many examples where a single sailing ship outfought and escaped from fleets of galleys that the continued use of galleys seems strange.

One example occurred in 1631 when small single-decked sailing vessel of about 100 tons, with ninety men aboard and a few small cannon, was attacked by eight Turkish galleys. A ten-hour fight followed. By throwing grenades into the galleys from the height of its deck, the crew of the sailing ship caused much damage and great loss of life to the Turks. They not only kept the Turks off, but forced them to retire in defeat. Another was in 1665 when a Turkish fleet of thirty-three galleys surprised a Frenchman, Cavalier d'Hoquincourt, commander of a sailing ship, in Porto Delfino on the island of Chios off the coast of present-day Turkey. The French ship drove off the Turkish galleys with cannon, swivel guns, and grenades. There were many such encounters reported in the Mediterranean, and gradually the corsairs did switch to the use of sailing ships, which included polaccas, xebecs, and other fast lateen-rigged craft. But even well into the 1700s they were still using galleys, as well.

In 1624–1625 it was estimated that Tunis had six great galleys, and fourteen sailing ships engaged in piracy. Tripoli had only two or three sailing craft using its port for the same purpose. But at Algiers there were six great galleys, and a hundred sailing ships engaged in piracy. The number of sailing ships at Algiers is deceiving, however, for the Algerians themselves still used galleys, while most of the sailing vessels were commanded by European pirates—Spanish, English, French, Dutch, and other nationals backed, frequently, by investors in their home countries. Even most of the Algerian galleys were commanded by Europeans. In 1588 of the estimated 35 galleys operating out of Algiers, 24 were commanded by Europeans. In another year, when 36 galleys and smaller galley-like ships were operating out of Algiers, all but 14 of these vessels were under the command of Europeans.

In 1638 the main fleet of the Algerian corsairs was captured by a Venetian fleet. The Algerian flotilla was compsed of sixteen great galleys, not sailing vessels. (These galleys used sail at sea, but during battle and at other times oars were used.) At the oars of these Algerian galleys were 3,600 slaves, or about 225 rowers to a vessel; thus they were large ships. They probably also carried about 200 soldiers who did the fighting when a vessel was boarded, and over a hundred seamen used when the galley was under sail. One hundred years later Algerian corsairs put out only eight small galleys and eight sailing ships.

Both the Barbary and the Maltese corsair fleets were operated as private navies. By their rules the Knights of Malta received ten percent of the money raised by the sale of captured goods at auction. Five percent was also to be set aside for material services, for nuns to pray for the corsairs, and to pay the officials of the order who

United States privateers, 1812. This type of swift top-sail schooner was one of the favored privateer vessels during the War of 1812.

looked after captured slaves and other corsair matters. The captain of the corsair vessel was to receive eleven percent, the crew and the shareholders of the ship were to receive the rest, with all captured cooking equipment to go to the ship's cook, and the surgeon aboard to receive all captured medical equipment.

Nearly all Maltese corsair vessels carried at least one priest. One time a Maltese captain took a captured woman into his cabin, and the priest aboard entered the cabin and took her out, much to amusement of the crew. The priest was able to go over the captain's head in this matter because it was one of the rules of the order that sexual molestation was outlawed. There was no punishment for breaking the rule, but the captured woman, once any of the crew had had sexual intercourse with her, was supposed to be set free.

The Maltese favored attacking convoys of Turkish ships operating between Constantinople and Alexandria. Sometimes their fleets stayed out for years. A fleet under the command of a knight of Malta made up of one Portuguese, one French, three Corsican, and three Maltese ships, is reported to have stayed out nine years on one cruise and four years on the next. The Maltese laid up their ships from mid-December to mid-March, usually at some port in the Aegean islands. In spring they operated in the northern Aegean, in summer along the coast of Cyprus, or off Alexandria. Late in the summer they moved to the Syrian coast where slaves were captured. The slaves were sold at Acre, Joppa, or under a white flag of truce in the port of Tripoli, or at Tunis. In autumn the Maltese corsairs returned to the places they had raided at in the spring.

Many stories concerning the Maltese corsairs were circulated in Europe during the 1600s. They told of some of the grim practices, as well as the rewards, of the corsair life. One story describing the adventures of a Maltese pirate told of the torture ordered aboard a captured Greek ship. Getting no information from the crew, the corsair captain threatened to kill the son of one of the Greeks if he was not given information concerning "infidel" cargo. The Greek seamen then admitted they were hiding three Turks ashore, to protect them from the Maltese. Going ashore, the captain captured the Turks and, since one was an important Turkish offical from Athens, he asked a ransom of 3,000 gold pieces. At Athens the governor personally handed over the money. He also organized games and a feast for the Maltese, and when a Turkish patrol galley appeared its officers and crew joined the party. It was all a very relaxed affair; ransom payment was a accepted fact of life to both the Turks and Maltese.

The booty of the Maltese was mainly cargoes of wood; this sounds unglamorous, but it brought a high price in Greek, Turkish, or Barbary coast ports where wood was scarce. Rice and lentils were also often taken, and sometimes cargoes of coffee, sugar, or linen goods. Captives were sold as slave. On rare occasions Moslem treasure ships were captured. These ships, with important personages aboard, brought a great deal of ransom money. If they were taken, however, the next year invariably saw a great increase of Turkish vessels on patrol, and war vessels sent against Malta itself, so their capture was a mixed blessing to the Maltese.

In the early 1700s European trade in the Near East became more important, and the sultan brought pressure to bear on European governments to curb Maltese piracy. This restricted the Knights, especially after Turkish captains were issued French passports, since it was illegal for the Maltese to attack any ships except those with Moslem papers. By the 1720s the Maltese were in decline, and afterward their raids were restricted to a few on the coast of North Africa. With the conquest of Malta by Napolean Bonaparte on his Egyptian expedition of 1798, the corsair activity of the Knights came to an end, and all Moslem slaves on the island were set free. Activity of other corsairs in Europe thereafter also came to an end.

The Moslem pirates of the Barbary coast did not winter-over as the Maltese did, but were at sea winter and summer. They raided mainly in the western Mediterranean, and in the Atlantic as far west as the Azores, and as far north as Iceland. (As recently as the early 1900s Icelandic fisherman sometimes kept a watch for Moslem pirates, for Barbary raids among their fishing fleets were well remembered and feared.) They, too, often stayed out for long periods, although they sometimes made as many as four short cruises in one year. They developed a number of strategic retreats where they could go to "regale themselves," as one observer of the day put it, when they had been long at sea. The island of Forementara, off the Spanish coast was one such base, as well as places in Corsica, Stomboli, and the Lipari Islands.

European seamen sometimes were drawn to the exotic surroundings of the Barbary Coast where they took up the corsair trade, especially if times were economically depressed at home. Prominent among the European pirates of the Barbary Coast were several from Sicily, Calabria, England, and the Netherlands. Khair-ad-Din was the most famous European to join their ranks. Also well-known is the Englishman, John Ward, who was active for many years after 1607, and who retired to a palace he had built of alabaster and marble outside of Tunis.

When they were cruising, the Barbary corsairs were under the command of a captain (*rais*), who was chosen by the owner or shareholders of the vessel. The ships had soldiers aboard who were commanded by their own leader (*aga*). It was he who was in charge during the actual attack and boarding. The soldiers used bows and arrows well into the 1700s. (They were probably more accurate than the handguns of the time.) Any ship, licensed or not, using one of the ports of the Barbary coast as a base for the auctioning of goods or for fitting out, paid the ruler of the port ten percent of the money gained from the sale of booty.

Between 1569 and 1616 alone, 100 Barbary ships captured a total of 466 ships off the British Isles. It has been estimated that in the year 1608 as many as 500 ships based on the Barbary coast were operating in the western Mediterranean and the Atlantic. This pirate menace, as well as the increase in trade, attracted the attention of the English Parliment after James I became king, and it brought about the establishment of a commission to investigate the Royal Navy.

The commission recommended that thirty new war ships be constructed. The attacks on English shipping did not prevent English merchants, or Dutch and Baltic merchants, from selling the Barbary pirates munitions, pitch and other naval supplies. Many of the Barbary corsair ships were built in Europe, and much of the captured cargo was sold in European ports.

Nearly all land raids involving Barbary or Maltese corsairs were swift affairs; they were usually over in a single night. On the sea both groups resorted to the use of false flags to entice a vessel close enough to attack. Moslem corsairs dressed in European garb, just as Europeans dressed as Moslems to deceive those aboard a ship that might prove a possible victim. A captured vessel, or prize, was sent to a designated port under the charge of a skeleton corsair crew. At times the captured crew itself was used; this worked especially well in the case of cargo vessels in which members of the same family were part of the crew. (This often was the case on small cargo vessels since they were frequently family-owned and operated.) One of the men then was held as a hostage aboard the corsair vessel to guarantee the captured ship's arrival in a stated port. At times a captured ship was allowed to continue its voyage after the signing of a ransom note, or after payment of ransom by the captured captain. The note designated the time, place, and amount of money to be paid the corsair captain. Usually the amount agreed upon was considerably less than the value of the cargo and ship, for it was a great conveniece for the corsair to carry on business as usual at sea while the captured captain spent his time and effort selling the cargo.

The uncertainties and complications of the situation at sea were described by a Frenchman, Jean Thévenot. In 1657 when the ship on which he was a passenger came to the point off Mt. Carmel, the captain, who was Turkish, got in a small boat and went ashore. Anchored off shore was ship of Maltese corsairs. Thévenot and other Europeans got in a boat and rowed toward it to visit with their fellow Christians. At the same time the Maltese put out a boat, and when they met, the corsairs jumped aboard, pointed a gun at Thévenot's head, and demanded the Europeans' clothing and jewelry. Meanwhile, the Arabs ashore had stripped the captain. The corsairs took Thévenot prisoner, along with the others, including some monks. When the Europeans boarded the Maltese vessel, the captain promised to return Thévenot's clothing and jewels, but instead he was put ashore at Acre with only his shirt. When the Turks questioned him, Thévenot, despite his ill treatment, lied to prevent the Turks from attacking the Maltese vessel. He said there were two or three hundred soldiers aboard the corsair; actually there was a much smaller number. The Turks, hearing his estimate of the troops, let the Maltese ship sail out of the harbor.

The Barbary rulers considered their corsairs as military units at war on the sea with any nation that did not have a treaty agreement with them.[2] At one time or another Spain, England, France, Venice, and other maritime states signed such treaties with the Barbary rulers and paid "protection" money to prevent attack at sea. Sometimes the Barbary corsairs ignored the treaties. Venice, Spain, France, England, and others at one time or another bombarded the ports of the Barbary state involved when these lapses took place. The bombardments occurred to insure the carrying out the terms of the treaty, not to end the payment of tribute.

When the United States became an independent country, its shipping in the Mediterranean and eastern Atlantic was no longer protected by English treaties with the Barbary states. Abdur Rahman, the Tripolitan ambassador at London, mentioned this to John Adams in 1785. Adams, then the U. S. ambassador in England, was also briefed on the Mediterranean situation. Rahman told him that the Barbary states and Turkey were "sovereigns of that sea" and no country could sail those waters without first signing treaties of peace with them. Even before this the Sultan of Morocco had asked that such a treaty be signed when the U. S. brig *Betsey* had been taken by Moroccan corsairs in 1784. Such a treaty was signed with the sultan in 1786, but no tribute payment to Morocco was involved.

In 1785, however, corsairs from Algiers captured two United States vessels off the coast of Portugal and a number of American citizens were taken prisoner. Algiers had already asked for a peace

---

[2] The Barbary rulers included the Sultan of Morocco, the Bey of Tunis, the Dey of Algiers, and the Bashaw of Tripoli. The title *Dey* was given to the commanding officer of the Janessaries of Algiers who disposed the pasha in 1710. The title *Bey* meant Governor; it was also used as the title for a person of equal rank to a governor. The *Bashaw* was the head of government who was also a military commander; it was a variation of *Pasha*.

treaty with payment of tribute for "protection" of United States ships; but the United States government had declined to sign because its budget was so limited; it did not have the money to spare. Denmark and other small nations of Europe had the same problem. It was not the principle that these governments found objectionable. Far from it; for like the nations that had such treaties, government leaders in the United States were aware that the Barbary corsairs saw to it that unorganized piracy did not get out of hand in the area. Paying tribute, and ransom, too, guaranteed a highly motivated maritime police force in the form of Barbary corsairs, who attended to other pirates' being put out of business.

There was also a good deal of opposition in the United States against the building of a standing navy. The people of the frontier regions were especially opposed to a navy, feeling it was not nearly so important as a standing army. When members of the Federalist party urged that a fleet be constructed to protect our shipping in the Mediterranean, one opponent, Senator William Maclay of Pennsylvania, said that the "eleven unfortunate men, now in slavery in Algiers, is the pretext for fitting out a fleet to go to war," and he wanted none of it.

During the early 1790s American relations with Algiers worsened. When the Algerians captured eleven American ships and enslaved over 100 United States seamen, the American consul in Algiers, Colonel Joshua Humphreys, wrote: "If we mean to have commerce, we must have a naval force, to a certain extent, to protect it." In January of 1794 a bill for the construction of six frigates was presented to the House by the Ways and Means Committee. In a short time, $688,000 was appropriated by the Congress to build the ships; but this naval armament act was so strongly opposed that to placate certain senators an amendment had to be added stating that in case relations with Algiers improved all work on the ship was to be halted immediately.

Ships take a long time to build, and the Algerian corsairs continued to annoy American shipping. Therefore a compromise settlement was made with Algiers. In July 1794 our consul in Algiers was authorized to pay the Dey of Algiers $800,000 in ransom to free the American prisoners, and to promise an annual tribute of $24,000. Despite the peace, work on the frigates did not end, for the payment of the ransom and tribute had brought about a change in public sentiment. In 1796 President Washington said, "To secure respect to a neutral flag requires a naval force." In 1797 the *Constellation, Constitution,* and the *United States* were launched. (See Appendix F.)

Even after the launching of the frigates, tribute was still being paid to the Dey of Algiers in the form of naval supplies—approximately $24,000 worth of pitch, wood, cord, sail, etc. Once the settlement had been made with Algiers, other Barbary states demanded tribute. In 1801 the Bashaw of Tripoli demanded a half million dollars and an annual gift of $20,000. But now the United States had a fleet, as well as a Navy Department, so Congress rejected the Bashaw's demands and, in fact, went a step further and declared war against Tripoli on May 10, 1801.

United States ships were sent to blockade the port of Tripoli, and to "sink, burn, and destroy their vessels." During the remainder of that year, American ships attempted to blockade Tripoli and to escort United States merchant convoys in the Mediterranean. The squadron, however, was not large enough to perform effectively; besides, United States merchant captains disdained convoys. That

A United States frigate. This type of vessel was the earliest built for the United States Navy. Two of the original United States frigates still exist: the *Constellation* can be visited in the harbor at Baltimore, Maryland, and the *Constitution* in the Boston harbor.

winter the squadron was forced to return to United States waters, for the enlistment of seamen was limited to one year, and many of the sailors' enlistments were up.

In 1802 a larger United States squadron was sent to the Mediterranean. It proved somewhat more effective, but it was not until 1803 that the Navy, under the command of Commodore Edward Preble, engaged in serious combat with the Barbary corsairs and effectively blockaded and bombarded Tripoli. As gallant as the actions of the individual ships and men were, the year passed without a major move toward peace. During the winter, in spite of severe gales, Commodore Preble kept the harbor of Tripoli tightly blockaded.

In 1805 Tripoli was blockaded and bombarded again, and Captain William Easton with a handful of Marines and Moslem allies marched across the desert to Tripoli from Egypt, and captured the town of Derne. Going forward, they put the city of Tripoli itself under seige. Attacked on land and at sea, the Bashaw sued for peace. A treaty was signed in June of 1805. The United States paid a ransom of $60,000 for imprisoned seamen. In the United States the war with Tripoli was called "the war without victory," because the government was still paying an annual tribute to Algiers. Many irrate citizens, stirred by the often heroic acts of American seamen, insisted that Algiers should be "compelled" to surrender, but the Congress thought otherwise. The most important result of the war was that the actions of the Barbary corsairs forced doubting senators to realize, even if only half-heartedly, that it was necessary to build a navy, and it helped make United States naval officers more professional.

The tribute to Algiers was paid yearly until the beginning of the War of 1812, when it was stopped. When the peace treaty was signed with England in 1815, the U. S. immediately declared war on Algiers. Two powerful squadrons were sent to the Mediterranean. One under the command of Stephen Decatur, who had proved himself a hero in the previous Barbary War. On June 17, the day before Waterloo, Decatur's squadron captured the 44-gun Algerian flagship *Mashouda* off the coast of Spain. Two days later the 22-gun Algerian brig, *Estedio,*was taken. A few days later the American squadron anchored in the harbor of Algiers. Decatur sent word to the Dey that he had come to sign a new treaty, the terms of which were the end to tribute, no further hostile acts against United States shipping, the release of all American prisoners, and in case of war between the Unites States and another nation Algiers was to remain a strict neutral. An added condition, to set a precedent, was that the owner of the American ship, *Edwin,* was to be compensated for its capture by Algerians in the amount of $10,000. Decatur said in effect that the Dey must sign such a treaty or have Algiers destroyed by the squadron. Hours later the Dey's emissary was rowed out to Decatur's ship where it was announced that the terms of the treaty were agreed to by the Dey. Peter Potter, a musician on the *Spitfire,* a 12-gun schooner in the squadron, reported that "a regular blow-out" followed this news.

Soon after this, Decatur took the squadron to Tunis. There he demanded that the ruler pay $46,000 in compensation. Within twelve hours the money was handed over. Decatur went on to Tripoli where the Bashaw quickly sent out $25,000 to compensate for the recent capture of an American vessel. Ten Americans were released from prison and when Decatur demanded the release of two other prisoners who were Danish, they were also sent out. A year after Decatur's visit to the Barbary coast a combined fleet of British and Dutch ships leveled the city of Algiers. This reduced the Barbary pirate menace, which eventually ended when the French conquered Algiers in 1830.

10. Oceanic Piracy

The age of global piracy began with the systematic exploration of the oceans by the Portuguese. The sturdy caravels that sailed from the busy ports of Portugal to the Canary Islands and the Azores, and down the coast of Africa and around the Cape of Good Hope, set the European nations on a course of world discovery and colonial development. The consolidation of power in the hands of strong central governments and the wealth created by the new commercial revival in western Europe allowed for such oceanic expansion. More and more, trade in the Atlantic seaports of Europe became a world-wide enterprise. Such trade was made possible by the introduction of new vessel types and the rapid development of the armament industry after the 1400s. But piracy also went oceanic, introducing such well know figures as Kidd and Morgan.

Francesco Carletti in the *Regionamenti* (Chronicles) of his voyage around the world from 1594 to 1602 gives a vivid description of piracy at sea during this period. Carletti was a Florentine trader who traveled from Spain to the West Indies and from there to the Pacific. There he stayed in the Philippines and Japan before going on to the Portuguese settlement of Goa in India. He tells of his departure from Goa en route to Lisbon and explains how it happened that instead of arriving in Lisbon he eventually arrived in Zeeland (in present-day Netherlands).

Merchant vessel of the 1400s.

On Friday morning, March 14, 1601, the ship anchored at Saint Helena. Stops were necessary to replenish water supplies, get fresh meat and vegetables to help fight sickness, and to refit after the long spans at sea which were typical of such voyages. The captain sailed close to the harbor to see if it was free of other vessels. There were three ships already anchored there, so he followed instructions that he had and anchored off the tip of the island instead of entering the harbor.

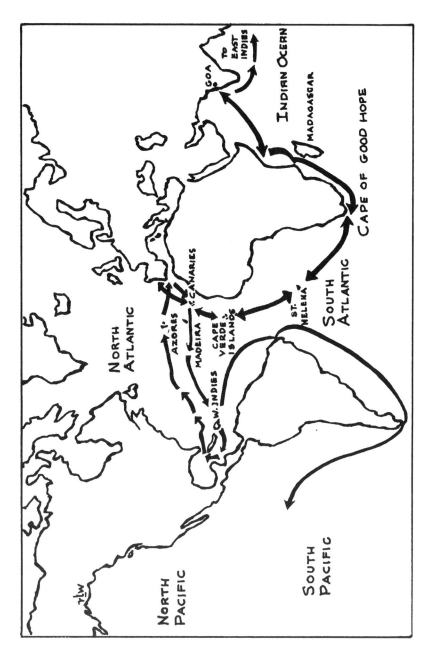

Major oceanic trade routes of the world in the 1500s.

Such instructions were commonly issued at the beginning of a voyage by a captain's government to alert him concerning political situations in various parts of the world. Another set was issued by the owners of the vessel telling him what action he should take concerning the vessel and its cargo. No matter the circumstances the captain was supposedly obliged to obey such instructions. They severely limited his initiative and often led to tragedy.

In this particular case the instructions read that if the enemy—the Dutch who were contesting Portuguese control of this route—appeared to be in the harbor at St. Helena, the Portuguese captain should "anchor at the point of the Paraveles, which is upwind from the harbor, from which the ships there would be unable to proceed because they would have a contrary wind." It might seem that it would have been more expeditious for the captain to ignore such instructions and continue on his way once he saw the enemy in the harbor; but this undoubtedly would have led to the death of many of the crew and passengers from scurvy, and perhaps from starvation. Along this leg of the Atlantic route to the Orient, places to land and replenish food and water were not easy to find. The route was discovered by Vasco da Gama in 1497. It went in an arc from Portugal to the Cape of Good Hope, roughly speaking, down the middle of the Atlantic far out of sight of land. The Cape Verde Islands and St. Helena were the two important stops in the Atlantic.

Carletti's ship had just anchored off St. Helena when two of the vessels from the harbor began to come toward them by tacking back and forth. In a few hours these ships were alongside and the men aboard them called across to ask if their "friends" needed anything at all. There was a babble of talk and confusion aboard Carletti's ship; should they trust these "friends" who said they wanted to be helpful? It appeared as if preperations aboard these supposedly friendly vessels had already been made for boarding. Then again, they might be honest men.

Suddenly, aboard the "friendly" vessels there was a blasting of trumpets and the beating of drums, the signal to the crews to get into battle formation. There seemed little doubt now; they had come to capture the vessel. "To arms! To arms!" shouted the men aboard Carletti's ship, with much yelling and running to prepare for the battle. Hastily the captain fired a piece of artillery, and the enemy responded, as Carletti wrote, "at the ratio of one hundred to one." All day the two ships blasted the Portuguese vessel causing much damage to the superstructure and a good part of the rigging.

During the night, when the cannon fire ceased, the ship tried to slip away from its attackers in the dark. The anchor cables were cut so as to make no noise by weighing the anchor. Also in the dark the crew unfurled the sails. But the attacking ships followed and the next day, one on each side, they began to pound the Portuguese once more with their "accursed" artillery. One of the "bombardiers," a Genoese, was killed on Carletti's ship.

The death of this gunner left no expert artillery men on board; of all the crew, he had been the only one who could handle a gun. Carletti does not mention it, but this came about because the position of gunner was *bought* before the voyage. People paid a great deal for the position, because the crew was allowed to carry cargo as part of their pay, making enormous profit, and the greater the rank of the crewman the more cargo he was allowed to stow aboard. It was not necessary to know how to use artillery to be classed a gunner on such Portuguese vessels.

The tragic result was that once the gunner was killed the enemy was offered no further resistance from the guns. Night came again and the passengers and crew waited through it without eating or sleeping because of the strain. They did not know what would happen to them when dawn came. Would they be tortured, thrown overboard to drown in the vast ocean—for they were far away from St. Helena by now—or would they all be killed outright?

It was March 16th, supposedly a festive day, for this day commemorated the capture of the notorious Indian Ocean pirate, Cunyale, who had been taken the year before. His head had been cut off and his body cut into quarters, the four parts being impailed on the city gates of Goa. But instead of festivities the bombardment began again, for the third day.

Before this the pirates had tried to hit the rigging and destroy the masts. Their ammunition was chained balls, used to damage and disable the ship without sinking it. Now, however, massive round shot was being fired. Seeing that they could not capture the vessel, they began to aim below the water line. This often forced surrender because of the threat of sinking. They succeeded in blowing holes in

A caravel—a common merchant vessel of the 1500s.

the ship. Water poured in and began to fill the hold. The ship was sinking. The passengers pleaded with the captain to surrender, hoping for reasonable treatment. The captain hesitated, then finally gave the signal that he was defeated.

The pirates boarded, took all the jewels aboard—diamonds, pearls, and rubies. The value of these jewels was estimated at "3,000,000 scudos," a great fortune. Carletti lost a valuable cargo of musk and gold, but he was at least taken off the sinking vessel when he proved that he was an Italian, and not Portuguese. The others were ordered to remain aboard their leaking ship until something could be done—in effect they were left to sink and drown. But the bales of pepper in the hold began to act as a plug, and the ship floated through another night.

When morning came they were told to jump into the water and be picked up by small boats the pirates furnished. Many drowned because they could not hold out until they were picked up; many were killed because the small boats were filled up quickly and the pirates would not allow others already in the water to climb aboard. They stood with swords in hand and killed any one attempting to get aboard, and they cut off the fingers of those who tried to hold on.

Actually these deaths were avoidable, for the Portuguese vessel stayed afloat until it was towed to an unpopulated island off the coast of Brazil where it was repaired. The Portuguese who had sur-vived were left behind, each with only a shirt and pair of pants. All merchandise and jewels were taken. Carletti was carried to Zeeland and released, minus his goods, money, and clothing.

Carletti's adventure points up many salient facts concerning pirate engagements at the time, especially the length of time they took. Usually pirates did not suddenly appear and board; they had to track a vessel slowly on the ocean. Often an intended prize would escape at night, or with changing weather conditions. This was true of oceanic piracy from the 1500s to the 1800s.

Local or coastal piracy using small oared vessels, sometimes with auxiliary sail, was a different matter. In one part of his Chronicles, Carletti tells of his ship being attacked by the inhabitants of a Pacific island as the vessel passed. The attackers used small, oared craft. In a report in 1882 Heinrich Schliemann, who was then engaged in his archeological studies of Troy, indicates that there was not a single village on the seacoast of the Mediterranean from Alexandria to Cape Lectum because pirate gangs used the creeks and inlets as bases to attack coastal settlements and fishing vessels. Such pirates used small, oared vessels. The Dyaks of Borneo used similar vessels that they hid simply by sinking them in shallow water when the authorities came after them.

The type of vessel that Francesco Carletti was on when he was captured by pirates.

The great improvement in guns and ships during the 1400s was one factor responsible for the success of oceanic piracy. The vessels Carletti traveled on were large. They were carracks and galleons, carrying hundreds of people and heavily laden with cargo. They were far different from the simple oceanic craft of the Norse and the Hanseatic League. Ships had changed drastically now that they were being built to withstand the rigors of the ocean, and now that the ship-building traditions of the North and South had merged.

A good part of this merger took place because of expanding north-south trade; vessels from Genoa and Venice sailed to London and Burges; traders from the Baltic also used these ports; northern and southern seamen often met. In addition, the Crusades (seven of them between 1096–1270) brought the warriors, pilgrims, and seamen of the north into contact with those of the south. The Mediterranean fleets were almost always used as troop and supply vessels, and as transports for pilgrims.

Coming into contact with the ships and maritime traditions of the Mediterranean, the oceanic peoples of Europe learned a great deal about sail and mast placement. As a result, the use of lateen sails (running fore-and-aft) became common on northern vessels. On northern ships they were placed toward the stern which made the vessels more maneuverable at sea. They still carried square sail running from side to side, but now the ships usually had more than a single mast forward of the lateen sail, for northern seamen had observed how well the many-masted Mediterranean vessels operated.

A strong stern rudder was used on northern vessels in place of the former steering oar at the side. In rough open water, if the wind blew with any force the side oar was lifted out of the water and the vessel was left floundering. A stern rudder allowed the ship more of a solid hold, or grip, on the water's surface. The stern rudder became a part of southern vessels that sailed into the rough Atltantic.

The vessels that emerged were the swift caravels in Portugal and Spain, and other Mediterranean areas; the carracks of the north (also built after a while in the south) with high castles both fore and aft, and the swift galleons that in many ways were a combination of these two types. The carrack, probably named for the Moslem *qurqār* (merchant ship) was much larger than earlier single-masted vessels. The temporary fighting castles used in earlier centuries were now completely incorporated into the body of the carrack, which now carried three masts. The galleon was a sleek, slender, three-masted war-merchant vessel.

Hosts of these vessels sailed to the Atlantic trade centers, and these centers dominated Europe more and more because of the wealth brought from oversea possessions. This flow of wealth was made possible not only by the new types of vessels, but also because of the dramatic improvement in armament aboard ships and on land. More and better cannon were produced in Europe than in any other part of the world. Bronze guns shooting balls of iron were in use as early as 1326 in Europe. As the years passed vessels more and more came to be equipped with armament. In 1380 the Venetians used bombards (mortars) on some of their vessels. During the 1400s the bombards gave way to cannon, and archers gave way to gunners with swivel guns.

In the 1400s the cannon were usually situated on the uppermost deck and holes were cut in the gunwale through which the shot went. Then in the early 1500s an important new approach to the place-ment of cannon was introduced—portholes were cut into the vessel's side below deck and the cannon placed below deck from stem to stern and on a number of decks. This allowed for a broadside of cannon fire during an attack, giving the vessel a great deal more power than those that were armed on the upper deck only.

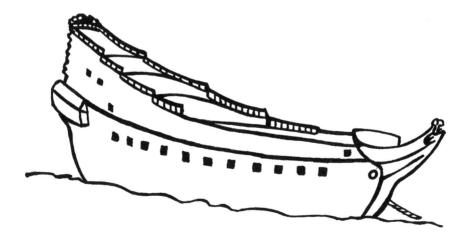

Gunports and decks on a galleon (shown without its masts or sails) of the early 1600s.

During the 1300s and 1400s guns had been thought by most tacticians to be a deplorable invention, for they were ineffective and dangerous in use. But by the 1500s cannon were so improved that they were being extolled as one of the three greatest discoveries made by man, the other two being the mariner's compass and printing. The advanced types of ship that went to the Orient and to the Americas had weaponry unmatched in the world. These merchant-warships, as well as the European men-of-war that developed from them, enabled the European nations to control many of the world's trade routes.

Where the shipping was, there also were the pirates. They used the same techniques to capture prizes that naval vessels used to win victories at sea. For a detailed picture of the "chase," as the hunt and capture of a prize was called, the book *A Sea Grammar, with the Plaine Exposition of Smiths Accidence for Young Seamen,* by Captain John Smith, is especially helpful. Printed in 1627, it gives a clear idea of how both pirate and privateer operated at the time. Smith began his account by explaining that the ship used should "saile well, yet [be] strongly built." The men should be experienced, and the crew should be more than adequate. He did not mention the reason for this, but it is obvious—there was a high mortality rate

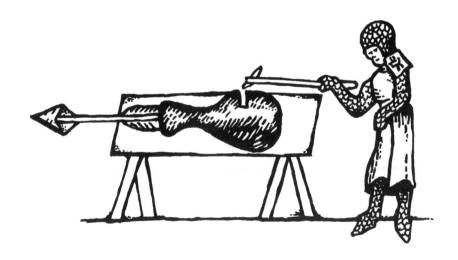

Primitive cannon, 1326.

during boarding; and besides extra men were needed to man a captured vessel to sail it to port where it and its cargo could be sold.

He noted that a good sailing vessel, well equipped with weapons
and having a knowledgeable crew, was usually "a Pirate, who are
commonly the best manned—but they fight only for wealth, not for
honour nor revenge." The first man to sight the sail of a vessel that
proved, eventually, to be a prize was rewarded according to the
custom of that particular ship. Sometimes a good set of new clothes
was given to the man who raised the cry of a sail on the horizon, and
at other times "so much money as is set down by order."

Before describing the actual chase, Smith offered some amusing
words of wisdom. "When we see a ship alter her course, and use all
means she can to fetch you up, you are the *chase,* and he the
chaser." For the chaser the first thing to do was to go the shortest
way, and the quickest. In this the best route was to windward because "you cannot board him except you weather him" (that is,
unless you get to windward of the chase, the side toward which the
wind is blowing. In this way your ship is constantly being forced
toward the ship being boarded).

"Board and Board," Smith wrote, "is when two ships lie together
side by side." If the captain of the other vessel knows how to defend
himself he will work his ship around to point it in such a way that
the boarder is forced to come on board at the stern end, the highest
part of the ship. From this point the defender can "do you much
hurt with little danger, except you set him afire." The best place to
board was at the bow. "But you must be careful to clear the decks
with burning grenados, fire-pots" and other similar weapons. Fire-
pots were explosive charges filled with powder, stones, and pitch.
Grenades, fire-arrows to burn sail, and fire-pikes to stick in the hull
to burn the ship itself all were used. Large fire-pots, Smith mentioned, "in a crowd of people will make incredible slaughter." Grappling and the use of "shear hooks"—hooks shaped like sickles
attached to the ends of the yard arms to cut rigging as one ship
passed another—were used in such encounters.

Pirates and privateers both used these methods of chasing and
boarding. The prevalence of pirates and privateers, both coastal and
oceanic, made the life of the ordinary seaman working merchant
vessels difficult and perilous. Edward Coxere, writing about his

adventures at sea from 1647 to 1685 told what it was like to be a seaman in Spanish, English, and Dutch merchant ships of the time. On one voyage they set sail in the Mediterranean with a cargo of currents and wine. "After we had been three or four days at sea, we spied a ship which made toward us." The ship gave chase all that day and through the night. At dawn it was near enough so that Coxere could see the ports open and the guns run out. Soon the attack began

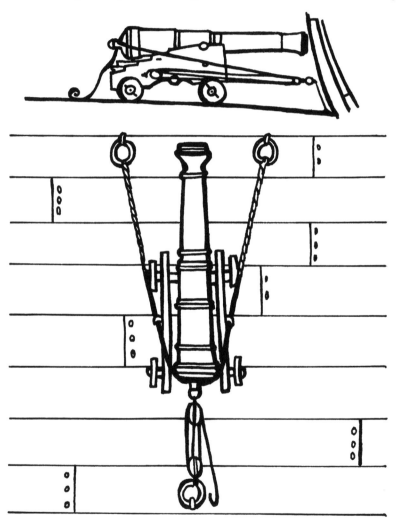

Two veiws of a naval cannon of the 1700s.

and surrender was a foregone conclusion because of the pirate's superior gun power and because there were only ten able-bodied men to fire cannon on the merchant vessel. Of these some were killed, Coxere himself wounded, and the quarter-deck almost all torn up in the attack.

"We, not being able to hold the dispute with him any longer, was forced to yield to these unreasonable barbarians, to whom we became their slaves, a heart-breaking sorrow." The pirate ship was called the *Vice-Admiral of Tunis.* Coxere was held a slave for five months at Tunis; his brother who had also been captured in the engagement was released for a ransom of 800 pieces of eight after two months, for in Tunis he had friends who were merchants from Italy. On March 29, 1658, the English paid 11,400 pieces of eight for the release of English prisoners at Tunis; Coxere was one of these. There were seventy-two men and boys, and two women. "Some had been there under bondage five years, some ten; one old man had been there thirty-two years. . . ."

On release, Coxere decided to ship out on a Dutch vessel that was going to the Canary Islands laden with beeswax, shelled almonds, goat's skins, and gold. Not far from the Canaries a ship was seen in the distance. Not knowing if it were friend or enemy, the captain altered course at night thinking to lose the chaser during the dark hours. He succeeded, but just as the ship was on the last leg of the voyage the same vessel appeared, overtook them and began to fire. The pirate captain had perceived that Coxere's vessel would still head for the Canaries after its course had been altered, so he dashed ahead and intercepted it.

After surrendering their ship, the Dutch discovered that the pirate was a Spanish ship. Coxere lost to the Spanish his chest and clothes—the very same chest he had plundered out of a Spanish ship not long before. There were other encounters with pirates, privateers, and men-of-war during his career as a seaman aboard merchant vessels, but these examples show how common such experiences were during those late centuries under sail. The wonder is that Coxere escaped with his life.

In oceanic piracy, however, it was not until the 1700s that passengers and crewmen were often wantonly murdered aboard ves-

In ancient times survivors of a pirate encounter who attempted to swim to shore were frequently followed in boats and murdered. This was a practice in modern times also, as depicted in this 1800 woodcut.

sels captured at sea.[1] The reason for this was that piracy in its last days fell into two separate catagories that were entirely different in purpose and technique. Some pirate vessels usually worked alone. These were the free-ranging pirates whose efforts to form large fleets inevitably led to disagreement and misadventure, for theirs was a debauched and disorganized existence. An example was the attempt of John Cook to form a pirate fleet in the Pacific in 1683–4. The

---

[1]During the 18th and 19th centuries, because of the outlawing of slavery and of the importation of slaves in many countries, death at sea increasingly became the fate of pirates' captives. (In Virginia in 1778 a bill was enacted outlawing the importation of slaves from Africa. This was part of the trend throughout the western world to limit or abolish slavery.) When captives could not be sold as slaves, hence subdued and silenced, pirates often reasoned that "dead men tell no tales." By killing their captives, they left no witnesses to testify against them in court.

purpose was to seize Spanish treasure being shipped from Lima to Panama; but the attempt was an utter failure. Pirate ship ended up fighting pirate ship, and pirate captains and leaders quarreled and killed each other. Such pirates were often termed "mad dogs," an appropriate name.

While such pirates murdered and devastated without restraint, privateers were often of a different character, and privateering usually attracted a different and more humane type of individual. Father Labat, a priest in the West Indies from 1693 to 1705, gives an interesting description of life among French privateers. At times he even went to sea with them, especially when he was assured that the voyage was peaceful in intent. On one such voyage, however, the captain and crew decided to raid a small settlement in hope of securing money. The ship was anchored between two islands where it lurked in hiding all day, for the raid was to take place during the night, as most such pirate and privateering raids did.

Toward sunset a sail was sighted at sea; the privateers could not restrain themselves and the chase was on. The unsuspecting intended prize was followed all night; in the morning the French privateers raised false colors. The other vessels an English merchant ship, came close to exchange news. Suddenly the French delivered a broadside bombardment, and after a brief engagement the merchant captain surrendered. The ship was boarded without further battle, and together the two vessels sailed for St. Thomas. On the way ransom arrangements were made, and a contract was drawn for the return of the vessel to its captain upon payment of a specified amount of money. After the papers were drawn up and signed the English captain was invited to dinner aboard the French privateer. He accepted, and after a congenial meal, with much toasting and drinking of wine, the vessels went their separate ways. The English vessel was released in its captain's care before the ransom was paid. It probably was paid, since this was a "gentleman's" agreement.

Labat tells of many strange things, mentioning that the churches of the French were beautified by ornaments supplied by privateers when they had sacked a Spanish town or captured a ship. These presents were acceptable to an honorable man like Labat simply because they were considered spoils of war. The French and English often raided each others' shipping in the West Indies; but the major reason that privateering was such an enormous endeavor there was that the Spanish enforced a complete prohibition against both French and English vessels except those having licenses from the Spanish government. This was true throughout the waters of Spanish-controlled South and North America, as well.

This arrangement originated early in the 1500s when the Pope declared that only Spain and Portugal could trade in the New World. This decree by the Catholic Church in Rome carried no weight in England which was Protestent from the mid-1500s onward. Other nations also considered it an illegal arrangement. A privateering war ensued against Spain and Portugal in the Americas.

The English privateers who raided in the West Indies during this period became great heroes at home, and since have been written about so often that a mis-interpretation of the greatness of Elizabethan sea power has sometimes been the result. England was not an important maritime nation at the time of the first pirate excursion by Englishmen into Spanish-American colonial waters. Sir Francis Drake (1543–1597), and other raiders of the time operating in the Atlantic and Pacific Oceans were not part of a large, well-oranized naval force. After the raids in the West Indies and elsewhere by such folk-heroes as Drake and John Hawkins in the 1560s, England "became a receiving house for stolen property", as Brian Tunstall so aptly put it in his *Realities of Naval History*. Queen Elizabeth I could not afford to maintain a large scale naval force, and so encouraged private individuals and joint-stock companies to organize pirate raids through the 1570s and 1580s, and later.

When Henry VIII died in 1547 the English fleet was strong, though not so strong as Spain's under the Hapsburg Charles V; nor was England's sea force as well-organized and powerful as Venice's which, with its great naval docks and arsenals, commanded great respect at sea. Nevertheless, Henry VIII had built up a strong fleet.

During the rule of his son, Edward VI, from 1547 to 1553, and that of his daughter Mary Tudor from 1553 to 1558 the English navy was greatly neglected. And Elizabeth I, who reigned from 1558 to 1603, with slender resources at her disposal was not able to build and maintain a strong naval force. Quite possibly she never quite grasped the importance of sea power, for the queen ignored her advisors when they repeatedly tried to get her to build up the fleet—she encouraged piracy instead.

Drake's voyage of piracy in 1585 was a typical English privateer's adventure of the time. It was financed by a joint-stock company, with London merchants and Elizabeth I both contributing money. Of the nineteen ships involved (not men-of-war, but merchant vessels), the Queen provided two, the *Aid* and the *Bonaventure*. The smallest vessel, named the *Duck,* was less than 60 tons. Using these ships Drake plundered Vigo in Spain, attacked the Cape Verde Islands, crossed the Atlantic, sacked Spanish cities of the Caribbean, and finally returned to England with plunder and ransom money. The adventure had cost £60,000 to finance, the booty totaled £67,000, a gain of only £7,000 to be divided amongst the participants. It was hardly a great financial success, but Drake did manage to harass the Spanish.

Another incident of Elizabethan privateering is described by J. E. Neale in his biography, *Queen Elizabeth I.* He relates that in 1592 a privateering syndicate operating in the Azores, in which the queen was a participant, captured a great carrack from the East Indies. The English, in their hunt for spoils during the night, inadvertently set fire to the ship from their candles. The chief officer of the group was said to have grabbed up £10,000 worth of plunder, and the jewels, gold, silks and perfumes seized probably amounted to nearly £100,000. Most of the men involved sailed straight from the Azores to the ports of England, where they smuggled ashore what treasure they could. When the news of the capture of the great carrack reached London, merchants flocked to the ports to quickly buy fabulous bargains: 1,800 diamonds, 200 or 300 rubies for £130. Elizabeth hastily sent Sir Robert Cecil to Dartmouth to recover what spoils he could for her, and the other principles who had paid for the undertaking had to be satisfied with the main cargo of goods. The queen also took the major share of this (it amounted to £141,000), much to the annoyance of Sir Walter Raleigh, a co-investor.

The privateers of England and France were like gnats attacking a huge lumbering but sturdy animal—the Spanish fleets. These attacks were irritating, annoying, and provoking; but against the vast resources of Spain and the fleets of grand galleons plying the Atlantic and Pacific, they were not seriously harmful to Spanish expansion or trade. The Drakes and Hawkins of the day were desperate, cunning, and destructive; but the courage and endurance of the Spanish in the Caribbean is often forgotten. The Spanish arthorities, of course, were concerned about English pirates—much as the United States in the 1960s and 1970s was worried about the North Vietnamese. But it would be absurd to claim that North Viet Nam was a military power equal to the United States. The analogy is not so far-fetched, for England was a small, undeveloped agricultural country; its position in the world of the 1500s could not compare with that of the Ottoman empire, the Hapsburgs' empire, or the Franco-Turkish entente.

Not until the reign of James I, Elizabeth's successor, after the peace with Spain was signed in 1604, did England begin to emerge as a colonial and an oceanic power. The basis for this development was laid by several shrewd moves made by Elizabeth's ministers in the very last years of her reign. The first was the incorporation of the Levant Company in 1592 (established in 1581), which traded in the Middle East; then the expulsion of the Hanseatic League from London in 1598; and finally in 1599 the incorporation of the East India Company, which controlled English trade in the East Indies. England was now on its way to becoming an oceanic maritime nation. Once peace was arranged with Spain, English shipbuilding greatly increased. But in the 1600s the Dutch and French were the paramount European powers at sea. The United Provinces of the Dutch had merchant ships with a tonnage almost twice that of England. In 1650 nine-tenths of English trade was being carried in foreign ships. By 1677 the French were as powerful at sea as the English and Dutch combined.

One reason that many people have an exaggerated idea of England's naval power at the time was the "defeat" of the Spanish Armada. This defeat at sea often has been reported in distorted fashion. Storms, Spanish mismanagement, misunderstandings between Spanish leaders, and several other reasons caused the Spanish Armada to fail in its attempt to invade England in 1588. The English snipped at the heavy Spanish vessels, which were loaded with soldiers ready for battle on landing. The English ships did not engage in a general confrontation, and they wisely stayed out of range of heavier Spanish guns. The English queen herself did not attribute the repulsion of the invading fleet to her seamen, but to God and His power to whip up up a storm.

By the middle of the 1600s England, Holland, France, and Spain all possessed islands in the West Indies. A pirate and privateering war at sea began between them and raged on and off through the next century and a half. This brief era in piracy has probably inspired more romances, adventure stories, tall tales, and serious works about pirates than any other period. Buccaneers, freebooters, filibusters, the Brethren, these are only a few of the names given to the pirates and privateers of this time. There is already abundant material on this period, much of it based on the often reprinted work of Alexandre Exquemilin (sometimes spelled Esquemeling, and sometimes appearing as John Esquemilin) who wrote *De Americanensech Zee-Rovers,* published in Amsterdam in 1678, with an English version, *The Bucaners [Buccaneers] of America,* published in London in 1684.[2]

During this pirate war that began in the 1600s, the West Indies trade was gradually dominated by British interests and protected by British war ships. British sea power of the 1700s slowly confined privateers and pirates to a few islands in the West Indies. After the 1720's English and American pirates were replaced by Spanish and French pirates. (Part of the privateering force of the Spanish was made up of the *Guardia de la Costa,* the Spanish colonial coast guard operating of the eastern seaboard of North America.) By the 1790s, with the British capture of many of the French and Dutch islands, pirates and privateers were deprived of friendly achorages. When this happened, the activities of many of the smaller pirate vessels, which could stay out only for a few days at a time, were seriously restricted. By 1807 only the islands of Cuba and Haiti were a real

---

[2]Other works discussing the period in detail are Charles Johnson's *A General History of the Pyrates From Their first Rise and Settlement in the Island of Providence in 1717, to the present Time (1725);* Johnson's later work, *The General History of the Lives and Adventures of the most famous Highwaymen, to which is added Voyages and Plunder of the most notorious Pyrates (1734);* and James Burney's *History of the Buccaneers of America (1816).* A recent work of value covering the era is C. H. Haring's study of the *Buccaneers in the West Indies in the XVII Century (1910).* An uncomplicated account of the period 1630–1720 can be read in Hugh F. Rankin's *The Golden Age of Piracy (1969).* This is to list only a few among the hundreds of books devoted to the pirates of the Spanish Main, the Caribbean, and the West Indies. Henry Morgan (1634–1688), Captain William Kidd (1645–1701), Bonnet, Rogers, Blackbeard (Captain Teach), and other pirates operating at the time have been the subjects of many biographies that are readily available.

threat to British control in the area. By 1810 Britain was in absolute control of the pirate situation in the West Indies except for the pirates based on Cuba where a weak Spanish government allowed them to operate without any curbs. (The governor of Cuba refused to allow the British to follow pirates once they had landed on Cuban soil.) In the early 1800s the United States Navy began regular patrols of the islands and the coasts of South America, a development discussed later in this chapter.

Some stories concerning the 1600 and 1700s are well known (see, for example, the Appendix, Women in Piracy), others, such as the feats of the Dutch pirate Piet Heyn, are rarely encountered. Piet Heyn, who began operating in the West Indies in 1623 and continued for many years afterward with much success, worked for the Dutch West Indian Company. He sailed with a fleet of about twenty-five ships in 1623, with 3,300 men aboard. One year he was audacious enough to capture the city of Bahia (São Salvador). In 1625, his fleet had grown to eighty ships that carried 1,500 cannon. In 1628 Piet Heyn commanded a special squadron formed to intercept the Spanish treasure fleet. Off Cuba this force discovered the treasure ships, and engaged them in a running battle. The Spanish galleons were finally captured, and the gold, silver, logwood, and other cargo brought 15,000,000 guilders when sold in the Netherlands. Interception of the entire treasure fleet that sailed yearly from Vera Cruz to Spain had been the dream of English and other seamen for generations; it had never been accomplished before. It is interesting that the unheralded Dutch, in their thoroughly businesslike way, should have accomplished this feat.

The great Spanish merchant fleets had come into being by royal decree in July, 1561. The decree made the convoy system obligatory. It prohibited any ship from sailing alone to or from America; if one was discovered the ship itself, as well as the cargo, was confiscated by the Spanish crown. Pirates and privateers could sometimes locate such convoys because they sailed the same general course every year. From Spain they left San Lucar, then sailed along the African coast to the Canary Islands. After a stop for provisions they headed southwest to catch the trade winds which carried them to the West Indies. Once arrived in American waters, ships left the convoy off their ports of destination; often this took place at night. Going back to Spain, the ships left from the Isthmus of Panama port of Porto Bello or from Vera Cruz, sailed to Cuba, then through the Straits of Florida to the Virginia Capes, caught the winds eastward to the Azores, and then to Spain. Pirate or privateer ships scoured these established trade routes, but their chances of meeting a convoy, especially one carrying treasure, were slim. The area was too large to be effectively covered, and schedules varied from year to year. But, like the submarines in recent wars, pirate ships concentrated their vigils in the waters close to ports of destination. A convoy might take a wide or varied course on the way to its destination, but once arrived it had to zero in on the port itself, narrowing considerably the area where its presence could be detected, and where attack could take place.

Esquemelin wrote on the manner of piratical operation of this period, and his words are interesting and probably fairly accurate, for he is supposed to have lived with the pirates of the West Indies for many years. "Before the Pirates go out to sea, they give notice to every one who goes upon the voyage of the day on which they ought precisely to embark, intimating also to them their obligation of bringing each man in particular so many pounds of powder and bullets as they think necessary for that expedition. Being all come on board, they join together in council, concerning what place they ought first to go wherein to get provisions." Their first job was to steal cattle or hogs from ranches, often killing "without giving any quarter to the miserable swine-keepers, or any other person that endeavours to hinder their robbery."

Once provisioned in this manner, another council was held in which articles of conduct were drawn up. (See Appendix E, Pirate Codes.)

> Herein they specify, and set down very distinctly, what sums of money each particular person ought to have for that voyage, the fund of all the payments being the common stock of what is gotten by the whole expedition; for otherwise it is the same law, among these people, as with other Pirates, "No prey, no pay." In the first place, therefore, they mention how much the Captain ought to have for his ship. Next the salary of the carpenter, or shipwright, who careened, mended and rigged the vessel. This commonly amounts to 100 or 150 pieces of eight, being, according to the agreement, more or less. ... Also a competent salary for the surgeon and his chest of medicaments, which is usually rated at 200 or 250 pieces of eight. Lastly they stipulate in writing what recompense or reward each one ought to

have, that is either wounded or maimed in his body, suffering the loss of any limb, by that voyage. . . . All which sums of money. . .taken out of the capital sum or common stock of what is got by their piracy.

They observe among themselves very good orders. For in the prizes they take it is severely prohibited to everyone to usurp anything in particular to themselves. Hence all they take is equally divided, according to what has been said before. Yea, they make a solemn oath to each other not to abscond or conceal the least thing they find amongst the prey. If afterwards anyone is found unfaithful, who has contravened the said oath, immediately he is separated and turned out of the society. Among themselves they are very civil and charitable to each other. Insomuch that if any wants what another has, with great liberality they give it one to another. As soon as these pirates have taken any prize of ship or boat, the first thing they endeavour is to set on shore the prisoners, detaining only some few for their own help and services, to whom also they give their liberty after the space of two or three years. They put in very frequently for refreshment at one island or another; but more especially into those which lie on the southern side of the Isle of Cuba. Here they careen their vessels, and in the meanwhile some of them go to hunt, others to cruise upon the seas in canoes, seeking their fortune. Many times they take the poor fishermen of tortoise, and carrying them to their habitations they make them work so long as the pirates are pleased.

Passengers and crew members who lived through the initial engagements in privateering encounters were almost always set free "on condition" as soon as possible. The conditions might include agreement to pay ransom, and a "gentlemen's agreement" not to fight against their capturers for a certain period. Unorganized pirates during these years often followed suit, only detaining crew members of the captured vessel if they were needed. Many times, however, passengers and crew were killed and mutilated, except for those who possessed special knowledge of the sea, such as a pilot, or a particularly strong seaman who might prove a worthwhile addition to the crew. These "forced" crew members were often put to various forms of torture in order to make them sign on the pirate vessel.

Even if prisoners were taken, as those captured by the pirate Bellamy in 1717, they were often later murdered out of hand. The killings in Bellamy's case took place near shore and the "doleful cries" of the victims were clearly heard along the beach, and later many of their bodies showing signs of severe tortures were cast up on shore. La Fitte (Lafitte or LaFeite), another celebrated pirate in these last years of piracy, practiced wholesale murder so that there would be no survivors to testify against him and his men.

At times prisoners were set adrift in small boats to make shore as best they could. With few provisions and miles from land they often did not survive. Another practice of the period was to cut all rigging, maul the masts, shred the sails of a plundered vessel and in this floundering condition allow it to go. It was not uncommon, however, for pirates of this period to sink or burn a plundered vessel. The only survivors then were those able bodied men who signed on as seamen in the pirate ship.

Tortures ranged from the cutting off of hands to round-robin beatings with clubs. In the beatings prisoners went in a circle around a mast and were clubbed each step of the way; at times broken bottles were used in place of clubs; and at other times, knives and swords. Walking the plank was merely a diverting amusement, and was not used as frequently as the more common practice of simply throwing survivors overboard, sometimes with a mock prayer. Tying a prisoner in a kneeling position in front of a cannon and blowing his or her head off was another mode of killing. The captives seem always to have had to face various indignities before death or release. Yet, such was the quirkiness of their nature that "free-ranging" pirates invariably believed they were hearty, good fellows, honest and trustworthy—although they did not even trust each other.

Captain Jacob Dunham of Connecticut describes what it was like to be the victim of piracy in the early 1800s.[3] His schooner *Combine* was seized rounding Cape Antonio off Cuba on October 13, 1821. A party of pirates boarded. Eight or nine men with muskets and drawn cutlasses in hand, each with a long knife and dagger at his side, comprised the first group to board. There were nine aboard Durham's vessel: the captain, mate, four crew members, two passengers and a cook.

The pirates numbered about 300 and had attacked with three small schooners and a sloop, plus a large open boat. Once aboard they forced the mate, sailors, and passengers into the forecastle.

---

[3] See Alden, *Lawrence Kearny.*

Captain Durham, who was weak from illness, was beaten severely and driven into the forecastle, after which the fore-scuttle (hatch-cover) was slammed. They all remained below deck while the vessel was searched; then they were brought up and ordered to sail the schooner near land and to anchor it.

The captain was promised the release of the vessel if he would give up whatever money was on board. He gave them nearly 500 dollars in gold and silver, all that was aboard, thinking they might take the money and leave the cargo and vessel alone. "After they had received it they broke open our trunks, seized all our clothes, taking the finest shirts and vests, and putting them on one over the other," Durham wrote. It is interesting to note how often free-ranging pirates fussed over the clothing aboard a captured vessel; it seems to have been an uncontrollable fetish.

Then they "hoisted the bloody flag, a signal for death." Durham was ordered into the cabin, forced to taste all the liquor to prove that it was not poisoned, then repeatedly threatened with death, being stuck, pricked and stabbed with a dagger over and over, and told he would be killed "by and by." When they had finished their play with him he was again driven back to the forecastle while the schooner was stripped of most of its sails, all oars, loose rigging, compass, quadrant, all beds and bedding and all the cooking utensils. The cook was taken aboard the pirate vessel: they evidently needed him as well as his tea-kettle and crockery.

The captain and the others remained in the forecastle. It was a terrifying experience, for after stipping a vessel pirates sometimes set it afire with crew and passengers locked below deck.

We remained some time in the fore-castle, when suddenly the fore-scuttle was opened and the mate called on deck, and the scuttle again closed, leaving us in the dark in a state of uncertainty. We soon heard them beating the mate; after the noise had ceased, we heard the word, "Fire," given with a loud voice, then after a moment's pause another voice was heard, saying, "Heave him overboard." I had a desperate sailor, called Bill, who flew to his chest for his razor to cut his own throat, saying he would be damned before he would be murdered by them rascals. The pirates had previously robbed the sailors' chests of all the articles they contained, and among them Bill's razor.

After a little while the scuttle was again opened, when they called for a sailor. There were four in the fore-castle, who looked earnestly at each other, when Brown, a favourite old sailor, arose and addressed me, saying, "Captain, I suppose I might as well die first as last," then taking me by the hand gave it a hearty shake, saying, "Good-bye." I told Brown to plead with them in the French language, as I thought I had seen some Frenchmen among them, and knew that he spoke French fluently. When he had got upon deck I heard him speak a few words in that language, but soon after we heard them beating him severely. As soon as they had finished beating him we again heard the word fire, and soon after, heave him overboard.

Shortly after, the scuttle was again opened and the captain was loudly called. I crawled up the scuttle, being very feeble; they then told me if I did not tell them where the money was they would serve me as they had the mate and sailor, shoot and then throw me overboard. I still persisted that there was no money on board, and entreated them to search the vessel. An old Spaniard was pointed out to me who they said was the commodore. I asked him what he wanted of me, looking him earnestly in the face. He replied, he wanted my money. I told him I had no money, but if I had I would give it to him; that the property belonged to him, but he had no right to take my life, as I had a family depending on me for support. Previous to this, the man who had flogged me before had made a chalk ring on the deck, saying, "Stand there," beating me with the flat side of a heavy cutlass until the blood ran through my shirt. During my conversation with the commodore, finding all my entreaties unsuccessful, and my strength much exhausted, I took a firm stand in the ring marked out for me, hoping to receive a ball through the heart, fearing if I was wounded I should be tortured to death to make sport for the demons. Two of the pirates with loaded muskets took their stand and fired them toward me, when I cast my eyes down toward my feet looking for blood, thinking that I might have been wounded without feeling the pain. During this time the man who had beat me before commenced beating me again, pointing aft toward the cabin door, where I proceeded, followed by him, beating me all the time; he forced me into the cabin, at the same time giving me a severe blow over the head with his cutlass. When I entered I found both the mate and sailor there who I supposed had been murdered and thrown overboard.

The rest of the people aboard were questioned and beaten, except for a young man, Mr. Chollet, a passenger who, for some unknown reason, escaped being beaten. The pirates then took off all the cargo consisting of coffee, cocoa, tortoise-shell, eight kedge anchors, and all provisions except part of a barrel of beef and about thirty pounds of bread. After another thorough search of the vessel (they even shifted all the ballast in the hold in their search for money), the pirates told the captain to "be off." There were only two jibs and the main-sail left to work with and few provisions.

As the schooner slowly made its way through the water the pirates were seen making themselves merry, while those aboard feared they might change their minds. Entering the cabin the captain found the cook who also had managed to escape. They sailed for nine days until they reached Havana where they took on provisions.

The pirate leader of this fleet was a man called Gibbs, who was later identified as James D. Jeffers from Newport, Rhode Island. It was a ploy of the pirates to tell their victims that their leader was someone like the Spanish sailor in this case, rather than identify their true leader. Gibbs, or Jeffers, later returned to the United States where during a brief period of wild living he squandered a small fortune. He was eventually apprehended, tried for the crime of piracy, and executed. Before he died he confessed to many acts of piracy, saying he had destroyed over fifteen vessels, in most cases killing all aboard. On one Dutch ship he killed all the crew and passengers, thirty of them, except for a young girl who he took with him. She caused such jealousy that her fate was discussed at a council of war among the pirates. It was decided that she should be killed. Gibbs gave the order to have her murdered by poison, and it was immediately done.

There is no way of knowing why Captain Durham's vessel was spared, nor why Gibbs and his men did not kill them all, as was their usual practice. The cook, while he was aboard the leading pirate vessel, noted that they had more than a hundred demijohns of "the best old Jamaica rum that you ever tasted." Perhaps they were merely too full of merriment and rum to be bothered with the few aboard the *Combine;* perhaps Gibbs felt lenient toward a fellow New Englander. Whatever the reason, Captain Durham and the others were unusually fortunate.

The new United States Navy began to play an important role in the West Indies in the late 1700s and early 1800s. Its first campaign was not against Algiers, but against French privateers in the West Indies. In 1793 France had declared war against Britain. (The Reign of Terror of the French Revolution was taking place at the time.) In April of 1793 the French minister to the United States, Edmond Gênet, arrived in Charleston, South Carolina. Gênet immediately began to fit out privateers to operate against the British in the West Indies. Much to his surprise the United States proclaimed neutrality two weeks after he landed. The French and many of the people of the United States felt this was contrary to the Treaty of Amity with France signed in 1778, which gave special privileges to French ships.

In spite of the proclamation of neutrality, followed by the United States Act of Neutrality of 1794, the French contined using Charleston as a privateering port. By 1795 the city was taking on a definite French flavor. There was a great deal of tension in the United States because of fear that the country might be drawn into the European war. The government tried to keep friction between the United States and Britain at a minimum. Yet, France had been of great assistance to the United Colonies during the struggle for independence, and many people felt a sympathy for the present French war. They saw no reason why grain from the mid-Atlantic states should not be shipped to France where it was sorely needed. The British naturally tried to seize all ships carrying grain across the Atlantic; they not only seized many American ships, but refused to pay for the captured grain. British war ships were also seizing United States ships carrying produce from the French West Indies, an important trade for the merchants of the young country.

The young American government was faced with a dilemma. To continue to help its former ally, France, would lead to war with Britain; to favor Britain would mean that French warships and privateers would be hostile to United States shipping in the Atlantic. John Jay was sent to London to try to arrange indemnity for seized U. S. goods. In November of 1794 he signed a very unpopular but very realistic treaty with the British. The treaty contained articles dealing with maritime affairs, and also provided that the British turn over to the United States outposts held by them on the United States' northern frontier. It stated that United States' ships trading in the West Indies be restricted to seventy tons or less; and it specified conditions under which such ships could conduct trade. One article was drafted to prevent French privateers from being fitted out in, or operating from, U. S. ports; it also stated that privateer prizes would not be permitted to be sold in the United States. As a result, by the fall of 1795 French privateers almost completely disappeared from the port of Charleston.

Because of the treaty there was a good deal of acrimonious feeling against the United States in France. The leaders of the revolution

Battle between the French frigate *Insurgente (right)* and the U. S. frigate *Constellation* in 1799. The battle, which lasted only about an hour before the *Insurgente* was defeated, marked the beginning of an American naval campaign that lasted for several months and gave American citizens pride in their navy.

believed they had been betrayed by a friend. American ambassadors were rudely treated, and United States merchant ships came to be regarded as legitimate prizes. Although the British had captured many of the French bases in the West Indies, French naval vessels and privateers still operated from several West Indies ports. When they seriously began to trouble United States shipping, the new American navy was sent to the West Indies to hunt them out.

The first engagement between United States and French ships in this undeclared war (usually referred to as the half-war or quasi-war) took place between the U. S. frigate *Consellation* and the French frigate *Insurgente* in 1799. In a little over an hour the French flag was lowered. The First Lieutenent on board the *Constellation,* John Rodgers, wrote, "Although I would not have you think me bloody-minded, yet I must confess the most gratifying sight my eyes beheld was seventy French pirates (you know I have good cause to call them such) wallowing in their gore." American ships took fifty privateers in this campaign, which lasted until September of 1800. Meanwhile

Napoleon Bonaparte had become regent of France under the title of First Consul, and he favored peaceful relations with the United States. To Europeans, United States involvement seemed merely peripheral; while to the citizens of the United States the satisfactory behavior of its new navy brought a sense of uplift and pride. (According to one British observer the American people were "absolutely mad" about these early ships and about the exploits of navy men. They did not realize that the behavior of some of the navy's officers was strange, indeed, and very unprofessional. When one captain was ordered to the West Indies to seek out privateers, for example, he calmly ignored these orders and cruised in the North Atlantic instead because he was afraid his ship would be harmed by a hurricane if he ventured into the West Indies.)

There were nearly three thousand piratical attacks in the West Indies and Caribbean between 1815 and 1823, encouraged by the governments of South America in their revolutionary wars to break free of Spanish rule. The South American pirates were not, however, directly under the command of such leaders as Bolivar and San Martin. Instead of attacking only Spanish shipping the "privateers" attacked all shipping. Up until the 1820s the United States government did not feel in the position to deal with the problem. Privateering was strongly favored in the country at large, for such acts had, it was felt, helped the young country achieve independence. Cruising instructions for United States naval vessels based in New Orleans as late as 1818 read:

> You will protect to the utmost of your power the commerce of the United States against the depredations of pirates, but you will not confound pirates with vessels duely commissioned which may be cruising against any *particular* nation, or nations. . . . Vessels legally commissioned as privateers, under whatever flag, are to be respected. . . [unless they commit] unwarrantable violence [on U. S. vessels].

Another reason for the lenient acceptance of privateers was that during the recent War of 1812 United States privateering activity caused British merchants so much harm that they raised a storm of protest with the British Admiralty. A strong anti-war feeling grew up among them. The reason is easy to understand when it is considered that in the last year and a half of the war Britain was losing an average of two ships a day. There were 526 registered United States privateers; of these about 200 saw extensive service. American privateers raided every trade route used by the British, including the East Indies. On one cruise in the North Sea two United States privateers captured forty-five ships valued at approximately two million dollars. These gains helped balance losses inflicted on American shipping by a strict British blockade of United States ports.

The problem of piracy in the West Indies, however came under attack in the American press. Trials for piracy were heavily covered. Details of various grim cases were headlined, with bold blockprints or etchings accompanying them. The Niles' *Weekly Register* (Baltimore) of September 22, 1821, just a month before Captain Durham's experience, reported, "Piracies of the most horrid description. . . are numerous off the coast of Cuba etc. . . . .these freebooters—the fag-end of what was recently called privateering—have become so bold our government has been spurred into action."

Sentiment in the rapidly growing ports of the east coast against the West Indies pirates grew to fever pitch. In 1822 the government began seriously to patrol the area. A squadron under the command of James Biddle sailed at will burning and sinking pirate craft. The following year the force was increased and vessels added for inshore work, to follow shallow-draft pirate ships, and to attack pirate bases on land. By 1829 over sixty pirate vessels had been seized, and many pirate bases destroyed. To a fair degree piracy was brought under control, but not until the Civil War, when swift steam sloops were employed as ships of war, did piracy come to an end in the region.

But privateering was dying out and soon would be outlawed by European countries, and piracy, with the spread of daily newspapers and magazines, caused horrified public outcries. The downfall of both came with the development of the steamship.

When the Declaration of Paris was signed in 1856 Europe adapted uniform maritime laws; privateering was declared unlawful. (It was not expressly denounced by the United States until 1898.) Such maritime laws could be enforced because navies now were capable of patrolling the oceans of the world. The English navy, one of the strongest of the nineteenth century, used steam vessels to end indiscriminate piracy. An early example of the power of steam occurred in 1837 when a paddle wheeler, the *Diana,* of the East India

Company, steamed toward six Malay pirate vessels against the wind and sank them all.

Pirates did not use steam vessels for the simple reason that they were much too expensive to operate and to build. Piracy was contained, then dwindled into short excursions with sloops and barques carrying very small crews. Steam vessels plying the oceans were, from the beginning, enormous craft. They had many specialized crew members who were necessary for their operation. The unorganized pirates of the time could not possibly compete with legitimate steam cargo and passenger carriers. And so the age of piracy came to an end. Although coastal piracy in some regions lingered, and acts of piracy were carried out from time to time, the vital trade routes of the world were free of piracy except as an unusual or freak happening.

II. Piracy in the Orient

Piracy in the Far East has often been characterized by American and European observers as being a more virulent brand than that encountered in the West. From the earliest European explorers to the latter day traders of the nineteenth century, the pirates of the China Seas have been depicted as more feared and fearful because of their practice of working in large, well-organized coastal and oceanic fleets. These fleets, each operated much like a naval force with chain of command and coordinated maneuvers, ranged the seas from Japan to the Philippines and Indonesian Islands, as well as far inland on the many navigable rivers of China.

Coastal piracy along the southern land mass of Asia, in the China Seas and the Pacific, no doubt existed from ancient times. Piracy on a large scale, however, did not come about in Asiatic waters until after the seventh century A.D. in India and the eighth century A.D. in China with the surge of development of oceanic commerce. Compared with the traders and pirates of the inland seas such as the Adriatic, Aegean and other arms of the Mediterranean, the Oriental traders and pirates covered great distances relatively early. In the late 1000s ships from Japan began to trade in Korea, and during the 1100s Japanese vessels were calling at Chinese ports.

Oriental maritime commercial missions were often piratical, with the exception of the trading ventures of the Zen monastaries. (Zen was a Buddhist sect introduced in China in the 500s A.D., and in

Japan in the 1100s A.D.) The sect's trade between China and Japan was peaceful because many of the Zen monks in Japan were Chinese. The situation paralleled the development of piracy in the earliest days of ancient Greece. Trade was carried on under the sponsorship of the feudal lords of western Japan, and it was usually under the immediate control of warriors on the trade vessels. If an overseas

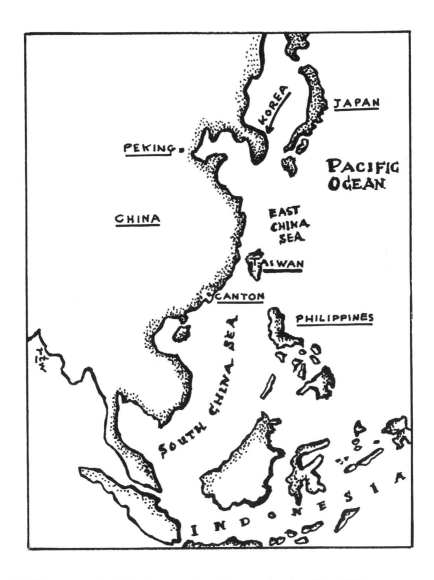

The China coast and neighboring areas where piracy continued until the 1900s.

expedition failed to turn a profit, or did not meet the expectations of the Japanese traders, or if the authorities of Korea or China refused to allow trade at all, as often happened, the warriors with their Samurai swords and arrows took to raiding.

As with the Norse, Japanese piracy did much to encourage trade on an oceanic scale because it modified the exclusionist policies of other Asiatic governments. It did not completely change these policies, but the threat of Japanese swords helped in the opening of ports. Warrior-traders increased during the 1300s because of the decline of a strong centralized government in Japan. The result was the formation of fleets known in history as fleets of the "Japanese pirates."

In Chinese records these pirates were called *Wok'ou*, and the Japanese called them *Wako*, both terms were roughly equivalent to stunted men, or dwarfs. In the beginning they were almost all Japanese marauders, and the first Ming emperor of China, Hung-wu (Hung-woo) who ruled 1368–1398, attempted to stop their depredations by bringing Japan into the tribute system. This system consisted of the payment of tribute in goods from "barbarian" rulers in exchange for gifts from the "exalted" Chinese emperor—in other words, trade with the outside world strictly controlled by the Chinese court.

Hung-wu at first asked the Japanese ruler to enter the tribute system so that trade, and in turn piracy, could be brought under control. He promised the repatriation of captured Japanese pirates and legal trade and support from the Chinese court. After a number of missions failed to bring about a tribute arrangement, he was writing in a different vain, saying, in effect: "You barbarian, why don't you behave. You're naughty and disloyal and your subjects do extremely evil things!" However, he was unable to establish satisfactory relations between the two countries. Formal tribute relations were not established until the reign of the third Ming emperor, Yung-lo (1403–1425), who arranged them with the Yoshimitsu shogunate in 1404. (Shogunate government was government by hereditary military dictators. "Shogun" came from *Seii-tai-shogun*, a supreme commander who subdues barbarians. The shogunate was separate from imperial government, which was ritual and civil. Shoguns controlled Japan for most of the time between 1192 and 1892.)

The tribute arrangement that was finally established was partly unrealistic in that it allowed entry into Chinese ports of only two Japanese ships every ten years. The realistic portion of the agreement was that Yoshimitsu, in return for Chinese copper coins and other "gifts," as well as trading privileges, would make an effort to control the pirates. But Ashikaga shoguns (1338–1573), of which Yoshimitsu was the third, were not in a strong enough position to really bring piracy under control.

Still, the Japanese seem to have sent six embassies to China between 1404 and 1410 instead of the agreed-upon single mission. The Ming later changed the agreement to three ships every ten years; but between 1432 and 1549 there were eleven embassies, some made up of as many as nine ships instead of three, as specified. This seems to be a better indication of the true volume of trade than the tribute arrangements, which were not strictly honored. But the Japanese shoguns were not able to control the pirates. Piracy increased and raids along the Chinese coast become more frequent.

Yoshimitsu did attempt to control piracy because of the financial aid the tributary arrangement brought him. He rounded up Japanese warrior-traders suspected of piracy and sent them to China for punishment. Still, the Chinese asked that more be done. His reply was that he lacked money because of the long continued warfare "in my humble state." In 1457 the Shogun Yoshimasa pleaded for financial support from the Chinese, writing, "As the records show . . . the Imperial [Chinese] throne [previously] made abundant gifts of copper coins to our state. Recently no gifts of this sort have been sent." (Fifty-thousand strings of money—50,000,000 coins—had been sent to Japan in 1453; but the pirate raids continued.) He went on to "urgently express" his "urgent hope" that this situation would be remedied. Then, perhaps, something could be done about the pirates.

Because of the many raids along the coast, the Chinese, as early as the 1370s, built an extensive coastal defense system connected by signal fires and strongly manned. It proved ineffective, however, against the sudden swift raids in which villages were pillaged and burned, and people captured, murdered, and raped.

The Koreans, too, tried to suppress the piratical incursions by forming an armada in 1419; but this fleet proved a complete failure.

Twenty-four years later, in 1443, the Koreans signed a treaty with the Japanese feudal lords of Tsushima. It permitted the entry of fifty Japanese trade vessels every year. Later the number was increased and the Japanese were granted the right to maintain permanent trading colonies in three Korean ports. These limited, but practical, agreements did much to control pirate activity in Korean waters by allowing the previously frustrated warrior-traders a legitimate market place.

The so-called Japanese pirates were not all Japanese; many Chinese from coastal areas joined their ranks. These Chinese were not merely simple seamen who worked the vessels, but active participants in raids and looting. During the later years of the Ming dynasty, which continued until 1644, Chinese were actually the leaders and major perpetrators in acts of piracy in Chinese waters, although the records still designated such pirates as "Japanese."

During the 1500s pirate activity increased to fearful proportions. In 1542 the coast of China was ravaged by "Japanese" fleets, as it was to be again and again. In 1552 pirates based on the island of Chusan attacked inland cities on the Yangtze and other rivers.[1] In 1555 there are thirty-four large scale raids reported in Ming documents. At one time during a general prohibition of maritime trade many seamen turned to piracy. The Ming rulers even tried to buy out the pirates with rewards and pardons, as well as by attacks on their strongholds, but the pirate assault increased. In 1560 a band of 6000 plundered in the southeastern province of Fukien. They appeared again in 1563 using Nomoa, an island opposite the city of Tenghai, as their base. Driven from this island they went to Taiwan.

During these years both the Chinese and Japanese pirates ranged freely through the area, raiding at sea, along the Chinese coast and

---

[1]Piracy on rivers has always been as common as piracy on the sea. The rivers of Russia, as well as those of the lands that are now Germany and France, were used by Viking raiders on their attacks. In the Orient, the Canton River and others have been favored raiding grounds for both Chinese and Japanese pirates from the earliest times. Tales of pirates on the Mississippi during the 1800s are part of the history of that river, and a part that includes numerous horror stories. Jerry McAuley, a famous river pirate on the Hudson River, became a religious man while serving a sentence for piracy in Sing Sing prison; when released, he founded the Water Street Mission in New York City in 1872, not with his profits from piracy, but with honestly-earned cash.

far inland. Only with the political reunification in Japan in the late 1500s did truly Japanese pirates decrease their activities. Before this they were often granted privileges by the lords of western Japan. One pirate leader was even allowed to use the port city of Hirado by the lord of Kyushu, and from this base raided far and wide over the China Seas. The larger raiding vessels carried as many as 300 men; with favorable winds they could sail from the Goto Islands off Japan nearly 500 miles to Ningpo on the Chinese coast in three days.

It may seem strange that attempts to suppress piracy in Chinese waters was so unsuccessful over the centuries. The explanation lies in the story of maritime development in China. The only period in Chinese history that was conspicuously oceanic was the early part of the Ming period, and it was unique. There has never been a strong Chinese navy. Fleets were raised during times of emergency; otherwise the oceans were, by the large, ignored as a base for military power.

Canal, river, and coastal activities have been the primary sites of Chinese nautical adventures. Chinese sea-power was concentrated in its fishing fleets and trading junks. China's one great oceanic naval war effort at any distance for the mainland of Asia was the unsuccessful attack on Japan in 1281 by Kublai Khan, the Mongol emperor. The great armada built for this invasion was destroyed by a typhoon, and the survivors were defeated and massacred on the island of Toka. Since there was no great Chinese oceanic navy in a true sense, there was virtually no gradual development of war vessels, and even in later periods, as we shall see, these were kept small. (In the nineteenth century the most talked of and expensive warship, a steamer, was not one at sea, but a monument costing wasted millions built in the Forbidden City.)

There had been sea raids against the Koreans in ancient times, during which the Chinese used single-decked vessels with deck-castles *(lou chhuan)* for archers. Also in ancient times, such vessels were used by the Chinese to raid in the south. These single-deck vessels had evolved from paddled canoes, but the main water transport of ancient China was in skin-covered coracles, wooden tubs, and rafts. One of the first pirate raids on the China coast, mentioned in ancient records, took place on sailing rafts used by the Lie Chhiu islanders. Sea-going sailing rafts were probably the antecedents of Chinese junks. Such sailing rafts did travel on open Pacific waters; they were made of bamboo and were very buoyant, and were said to be unsinkable even when heavily laden with cargo.

The oldest description of warships (as against simple ships used in war time), is found in an A.D. 759 Taoist military and naval encyclopedia. It may seem amazing that from the 8th to the 18th centuries A.D. no significant experimentation with war vessel types occurred in China. Perhaps it is not so strange, though, in view of the fact that China was a nation that warred primarily on land, not at sea. From the 700s through the next ten centuries descriptions of the same types of war vessels consistently reappear in the Chinese literature. There were the *tower ships,* which were rowed battle ships with three decks armed with catapults (which from about 1130 onward were used to hurl explosive bombs), and archers. The largest of these tower ships was classed as eight-oared. The oars were actually large sweeps, each manned by four men in calm weather. Then there were the *combat junks* which were less protected, single-decked vessels with deck-castles. The main strength of these warships were the "marines" based on them. A third type used during this thousand year period was the *sea-hawk* ships, which were converted merchant junks. *Covered-swoopers, flying barques,* and *patrol boats* were smaller fast ships. These vessels were not concentrated into a national "Navy." They were built and used by the separate provinces, but only in times of need.

A capacity for oceanic trade did not develop in China until the 11th and 12th centuries. Prior to this Chinese "international" and oceanic trade was mainly conducted by Arab and Persian merchants in South China. From 1086 onward, or at any rate after 1111 when the marine compass was first reported in Chinese literature, the Chinese themselves took to the high seas. Even then navigation was mainly centered along the coast. Toward the middle of the 1000s astronomical and marine charts began to be published giving sailing directions, soundings, prevailing winds and currents, depths, anchorages, landmarks, and tides; and during the late part of the Sung (960–1279) period, and the Yüan (1280–1368) and Ming (1368–1644) periods, shipbuilding techniques for constructing vessels to sail the oceans made pronounced advances in China; the result was the sea-going junk.

In the late 1200s Canton, which probably had a population that was half Moslem at the beginning of the 800s, was no longer the most important port for foreign trade. Ch'üan-Chou and Fuchow, on the Fukien coast, then dominated foreign trade. Chinese shipowners gradually replaced the merchants from the Middle East, although at Hangchow, the capital of China at the time, a number of Moslem and Jewish traders still did business.

From the 11th to the 13th centuries China experienced extraordinary commercial expansion. Chinese junks went to Japan, Malaya, the coasts of India, Bengal and Africa. There was a period of decline during the Mongol control of China, and then the highest period of oceanic adventure in Chinese history during the Ming period. Still, the most important Chinese trade was conducted by a vast fleet of coastwise vessels that kept the large trading centers on the southeast coast in touch with those of the south coast as far as Canton. The great sea-going junks did ply between China and the main islands of the East Indies, India and elsewhere during the monsoon season, but their trade was not on the same large scale as the river trade and canal trade. In the eastern part of the empire a great network of canals, the largest from 18 to 30 feet wide, linked the larger towns, and day and night carried an uninterrupted flow of traffic.

The reason for going into this matter in such detail as it relates to piracy in the Orient, is that piracy in China was conducted on Chinese rivers, along the coast and among the great fishing fleets of the country. It was conducted by pirate fleets, and was similar to that conducted by the Moslem countries. It was not oceanic in the sense of the oceanic pirate fleets of the English, French, and others. The long-distance merchant class was small, and the emperors of China were almost always predominately land-minded. China's was an alluvial culture in which control of the rivers was necessary; the system of water control, with dams, canals and terraces, was part of the way of life. Early Chinese empires stretched inland away from the sea. The T'ang dynasty (618–906), for instance, extended thousands of miles inland, past present-day Lake Balkhash in the Soviet Socialist Republic. The Mongol Empire (Yüan dynasty) with its capital at Peking, was even more extensive, stretching from the China Sea to Europe. In control of such vast and rich and varied land masses during much of their history, there was little the Chinese could not produce among their own peoples.

Chiefly during the Ming dynasty there was a strong move toward great oceanic international maritime expansion. Between 1405 and 1431 China launched seven great ocean expeditions. They extended as far as Somaliland in Africa and to the Persian Gulf (perhaps even as far as South Africa and the western coast of North America). Nevertheless, interest in long-distance oceanic maritime expansion and trade was not sustained. The times were prosperous and by and large unmarked by tumultuous events during much of the Ming rule, and after the 1400s foreign exploration and tributary trade was all but abandoned.

The lack of interest in oceanic maritime development and trade on the part of the Chinese emperors was frustrating to the Japanese, and this frustration led to piracy. If the Japanese could not trade with China, they would raid to get her goods. Such lack of interest was also frustrating to Chinese coastal mercantile groups who circumvented the official imperial policies by taking to piracy.

When in the 1600s the Ming dynasty ended, the loyal Ming follower, Cheng Ch'eng-kung, known to westerners as "Koxinga," took to piracy as a means of guerrilla warfare against the succeeding rulers. He set up his base of operations on the island of Taiwan and proved so effective that the new rulers moved the mainland coastal population inland so that he would be denied necessary supplies. Subsequently Taiwan became a haven for other pirate fleets. Although these were partially suppressed when the island was conquered in 1683, Taiwan remained a favorite pirate base well into the 1900s.

Piracy was a threat to the coast of China and to its seagoing junks all during the eighteenth and nineteenth centuries. The methods used to control pirates were ineffective and the efforts were decentralized ones, far different from those that had been employed so effectively by Pompey in the Mediterranean.

The emergency fleets that were occasionally built in China were purposely organized in such a way that confederation by the various provinces would be difficult, so that they would pose little threat to the Imperial court. Each coastal province built an independent "navy" of warships for coastal patrol duty only. They were trained in small, separate units so that no province could develop excessive naval power. Patrol and arrest activities were severely restricted; one province could not function in the waters of an adjoining one. This gave the pirates a great advantage; they could raid on land and sea in one area, then flee to a neighboring province and avoid arrest.

Another factor that prevented a successful campaign was that Chinese war vessels were small compared to the vessels used by the pirates. The ships employed by the provinces were only about a hundred feet long. They were light, manned with only about a hundred men, and they carried only a few cannon. Their size was regulated by government order, as was the size of trading junks. The purpose of these regulations was to prevent trading vessels from surpassing naval vessels in size. Despite these rules, it was not unusual for a junk to be three times as powerful as the government fighting craft, and to carry from two to four hundred men, and at times many more. Naturally pirates ignored the law regulating the size of a vessel, and their crews were often made up of as many as 600 men.

William Dampier, a pirate adventurer, in the story of his life written in the late 1600s, wrote that a junk of that time was "built with a square flat Head as well as Stern, only the Head or forepart was not so broad as the Stern." There was a thatch "house" on the deck used by the seamen, and the hold—amazingly modern—was divided into many small compartments, "all of them made so tight, that if a Leak should Spring up in any one of them, it could go no further, and so could do little damage. . . . These Junks have only two Masts, a Main-mast and a fore-mast. The fore-mast has a square Yard and a square Sail, but the Main-mast has a sail narrow aloft, like a Sloops-Sail, and in fair Weather they use a Top-sail." The watertight compartments were a feature of oriental vessels often commented upon by European travelers; yet they did not become a part of western ship construction until centuries later. Some historians believe that these compartments were developed from free-flooding compartments used on Chinese fishing vessels to bring fish to market alive.

These large trading junks, almost square in shape, with a raised prow and poop which were also square, had eight to ten pairs of oars (sweeps), two stone anchors, and sails of matting or canvas. The largest could carry five or six hundred people, and several tons of goods. The crews, composed not only of sailors but also of archers and crossbow-men, whose arms were put into storage at every Chinese port of call, had officers in charge of them. Black men (actually probably brown men from Malaya) did the heavy work on board. Each junk had to have a paper issued to it by a commissioner of merchant ships. The document was sealed with a red official seal, and it bore the names of the members of the crew, the dimensions of the junk, and information about the cargo.

After the Europeans began to trade in the Orient in the 1500s (Europeans had used Moslem middlemen before that time) pirate attacks were often directed against them, but the European vessels were sent out in convoy, and even alone usually proved too strong to subdue. Attacks on European-controlled ports like Manila, such as the one under the direction of the Chinese pirate Lim ahony (Lin Feng) in 1574, were, however, often successful. Pirate fleets grew so large that they were capable of attacking Taiwan in 1806 with more than 100 ships and 10,000 men.

Raids on land followed the same pattern in later centuries as in earlier times; they were usually hit-and-run affairs. Surprise, brutality and overwhelming fighting forces usually enabled the pirates to succeed on such raids. An English seamen, captured by Chinese pirates in 1809, described what a raid was like along the coast and up a navigable river. He was forced to work on one of the vessels until the English government paid his ransom. (If taken alive with no possibility of ransom the captive was either forced to join the pirates or was quickly cut to pieces. Many Chinese preferred death, for if government forces caught them working as pirates their families would be executed with them, since in China a man's family was considered an accomplice to any crime. Wife, children, parents, and even cousins and nephews were killed under this order of things, supposedly leaving no one alive who was related to the criminal, or who would attempt revenge for his death.)

The pirates who had captured the English seamen sailed up the Canton River. The pirate fleet consisted of more than five hundred vessels of varying size. The Chinese explained that their raid was being carried out to collect voluntary "contributions" from the towns and villages along the shore. There were frequent fights between the pirates and Chinese soldiers; the soldiers were always defeated. Some villages offered resistance, and these were ravaged and left in ruin.

One village promised payment on the return of the raiders down river, saying they did not have time to collect the money. Instead of money, however, the pirates received cannon fire when they returned, for during the pirates' absence the villagers had mounted guns on a hill. The raiders, however, overwhelmed the place and with much brutality destroyed it.

Of this time the records of the East India Company say, "In the years 1808, 1809, and 1810 the Canton river was so infested with pirates, who were also in such force, that the Chinese government made an attempt to subdue them, but failed. The pirates totally destroyed the Chinese force; ravaged the river in every direction; threatened to attack the city of Canton. . .and killed and carried off. . .several thousands of inhabitants." The men who refused to join the fleet after capture were either summarily hacked to pieces, of strung up a few feet off the deck with hands tied behind their backs, and unless they took an oath of alligance to the pirates they were flogged to death.

Such pirate raids went on well into the twentieth century, but they were considerably curbed by the introduction of armed steam vessels by European and American traders. One of the first, the *Nemesis,* was put into service by the East India Company. It was an iron-hulled steam frigate of 184 feet and operated with 120 horsepower; it had two 32-pounders on pivots at the bow and stern. Such vessels could out-fight and out-maneuver junks of all sizes. Using rockets and cannon these iron steamers, supported by the traditional wooden war vessels of Europe, could devastate a fleet of Oriental ships, as the *Nemesis* did early in 1841.

European steamship companies worked the routes of the Orient from the 1840s onward. This deterred piracy against western shipping, but it did not protect Chinese shipping. The modernization of Chinese transportation was slow. The first steamship company was not set up in China until 1872. Called the China Merchant's Steam Navigation Company, it dominated Yangtze trade for decades and put many traditionally junk-operated pirate fleets at a disadvantage.

The development of steam navigation took place in other parts of the Orient, also. In the Dutch East Indies and Borneo, both the English and the Dutch introduced steamers during the nineteenth century. This increased British trade in the East, and also helped to subdue rulers of small principalities and to suppress pirates. Among

The East India Company steamship *Nemesis* destroying Chinese junks early in 1841. Such iron-hulled steam frigates could outfight and outmaneuver even the largest wooden pirate vessels under sail.

these islands, groups of pirates cruised in squadrons, operating from forty to over a hundred and fifty large sailing vessels. These were assisted by smaller craft which sometimes made up fleets of as many as 800 boats crewed by thousands of men. One such fleet, used to attack passing convoys, was active in 1804 and contained an estimated 19,000 seamen.

The popular vessel for piracy among these islands was the *praus* (also called *prahus* or *proas*). Some of those were nearly a hundred feet long and could carry sixty to a hundred tons. They were operated under oars during pirate raids on shipping, sometimes with from fifty to a hundred rowers who were often slaves. (One captured merchant was held ten years in chains and forced to work as a slave.) Praus also had sails and cannon. They ranged from the Celebes to the Philippines, from Borneo to Java and Sumatra. Efforts by the Dutch and English to suppress these pirates in order to protect their own commercial interests led to conquest and rule in many areas in this region.

From earliest times pirates had appeared in the Red Sea and Gulfs of Persia and Oman, as well as in the Indian Ocean and its arms—the Arabian Sea and Bay of Bengal. Although the history of these pirates is of some interest, it is not important in an historical sense. As in China they did not help shape maritime policies, for there were no navies in the region. Even India, the largest and most important land mass in the area, could do nothing to suppress piracy. India was a collection of small states often conquered, consolidated, and then fragmented. It is no wonder that piracy was a prevalent part of the maritime adventures in this region.

Far back in history, European and Near Eastern governments took precautions against pirates of the Red Sea, Persian Gulf, and the Indian Ocean. Egyptian and Roman records both mention that archers were used on ships working in these waters. In 690 B.C. Sennacherib, king of Assyria, sent an expedition against pirates in the Persian Gulf. The Roman emperor Trajan tried suppression with a naval force in A.D. 116, as did Sapur II of Persia in the mid-300s. Caliphs of the great Moslem nations also attempted to control piracy in the area as early as the 800s, as the Portuguese, Dutch and English were to do centuries later—all to no avail until steamers were developed. The vessels used in these attempts were too far from their home bases for effective long-term campaigns, and the coasts of the area were extremely difficult to subdue with their shifting populations.

After the Moslem invasions of India, from the early 1000s to the early 1300s, there was a regular and heavy traffic between Arab lands and the subcontinent, especially the pilgrims to Mecca. Fleets of vessels carrying pilgrims made the passage regularly, and were often subject to pirate attack in the Indian Ocean. After the introduction of cannon these pilgrim vessels carried as many as sixty-two guns. They also carried as many as 400 musketeers, in addition to crews and up to 600 passengers.

Non-Moslem people have called these Indian Ocean pilgrim vessels *dhows* (also *dau* or *dow*), but this is a term that is not used among Moslems, who have no vessel they, themselves, call a dhow. A dhow was (and still is—these vessels are still seen today) any of several types of lateen-rigged craft with two or three masts raked forward; the larger dhows were sea-going. The name dhow has been applied for centuries to Moslem or Arab vessels of this area.

The favorite vessels of pirates in the Indian Ocean included booms, baggalows (baggalas or bughlas), and batils—all types of

dhows. *Baggalows* were large ships, sometimes up to 300 tons bur-
den, with high, square castle-like poops, with square port holes; they
were elaborately carved and decorated from bow to stern. They
carried enormous lateen sails, especially on the mainmast, and were
often crewed by 300 men or more; one reason for this was that it
took a good deal of manpower to raise the gigantic mainmast and
sail. *Booms* were ships of a very similar type, but with long straight
stemposts. *Batils* were also similar to baggalows but carried a lugsail
(a four-cornered fore-and-aft sail); they were favored in the Persian
Gulf and famous for their speed.

At times a large dhow carried as many as a thousand pilgrims.
Native (as well as foreign) pirates plied the waters off India and the
Arabian peninsula seeking out such pilgrim craft. The haul was
usually great—ransom, slaves, jewels and gold.

Marco Polo in the tale of his travels described the practices of
these pirates. The specific group he deals with are the pirates on the

A boom, showing the long straight stempost typical of this type of vessel.

Malabar coast, a district in southwestern India. "There are," he tells us, "numerous pirates, who yearly scour these seas with more than one hundred vessels, seizing and plundering all the merchant ships that pass that way." The wives and children of these pirates accompany them to sea. So that ships could be detected and captured their vessels were anchored five miles from each other, twenty ships stretching a hundred miles. On sighting a vessel a signal fire was lit and all the ships drew toward it. Polo reports that no injury was done to passengers or crews, but that they were taken ashore and released, with only the vessel itself and the cargo taken as a prize.

The last statement does not completely tally with Oriental and Arabian reports. Sometimes the passengers and crew were put ashore, usually in a desolate area, where many died of starvation or thirst. In other cases most of the people aboard a captured vessel were killed, many after atrocious torture. In the 1600s a system of ransom-or-slavery instead of murder became the general practice. But torture continued to be a feature of some pirate encounters even afterward, as well as murder. One captive in 1696 had his lips sewn up with a sail needle when he refused to remain quiet; his vessel was set afire, and although he was set on shore he died soon afterward.

Sometimes passengers were set adrift in boats. Oriental merchant craft usually carried many small boats, sometimes as many as ten to facilitate loading at the many places of trade where there were no port facilities. Those on captured vessels in the Indian Ocean were set adrift, as in the Atlantic, without oars, sails, or water or other provisions. Marco Polo's informants would not be likely to mention such practices to a foreigner. Polo does mention that "pirates of the most desperate character, who, when in their cruise they seize upon a traveling merchant, immediately oblige him to drink a dose of seawater, which by its operation on his bowels, discovers whether he may not have swallowed pearls or jewels upon the approach of the enemy, in order to conceal them." This was a common practice in all areas and eras.

From the 1600s onward the native pirates in the Orient became less and less successful so far as attacks on European trading vessels was concerned because the European ships could out-fight them, except for the most determined and powerful fleets or groups of pirates. Pirates still preyed on native shipping, however. Going in convoy European vessels could sail with a fair chance of safety, unless they were becalmed, in which case the oared native pirate craft had the advantage.

Another danger, perhaps greater than piracy, for ships arriving in the Orient from Europe was scurvy; it was not unusual for more than two-thirds of the crew to have the disease after the long voyage around the Cape of Good Hope. In such cases the crew could not handle the ship efficiently, nor defend it effectively. Oriental pirates, therefore, commonly attacked a European vessel on the last leg of its long voyage to test its strength. In such cases the fight would be fierce with even "the mission priests . . . manning the poop, sword in hand," defending the ship, as Abbé de Choisy wrote in 1685.

During the 1700s and 1800s piracy in the Indian Ocean went international, becoming part of the itinerary of oceanic piratical voyages. The scope of such voyages is interesting. A pirate ship might leave the coast of North America after raiding the shipping there; go to the West Indies and intercept merchant vessels passing between the islands and straits of that region; then, perhaps sail down the coast of South America and into the Pacific to harry shipping there; then across the Pacific and to the Philippines or the East Indian archipelago. Or, from the West Indies, out to the Atlantic islands, down the African coast, around the cape and into the Indian Ocean. Madagascar became one of the principal bases for the European and American vessels working "on the account," an expression that had simply come to mean piracy. The pirate headquarters in Madagascar was at the small island of St. Mary's, or at Antanavoula.

Boredom, heavy drinking, poor organization and little loyalty to either their pirate compatriots, fellow crew members or captain, or to the "oath" they took on joining a pirate group (see Appendix E) appear to have been common characteristics among pirates of the oceans. The careers of the pirates using Madagascar as a base were usually short, lasting only a year or two. In fact, this was the case with most oceanic pirates. During the 1700's one, a Captain Lowther, captured thirty-three ships during his seventeen month career; Edward Low took 140 vessels in twenty months; Captain Bartholomew Roberts took 400 prizes in three years. Aside from Morgan, who was active in the 1600s and who was perhaps more a privateer than a pirate, Roberts was possibly the most successful pirate of the period. He was a strict disciplinarian, and disapproved of strong drink and gambling. He ranged freely around the world until he was killed during a ship-to-ship encounter. Edward Low was noted for his cruelty, especially favoring cutting off the ears of his prisoners; after his short career and success he disappeared.

Even after the suppression of piracy in the Orient there remained successful fleets in operation in Chinese waters, but they did not operate against steamers. They plagued fishing fleets and traders sailing along the coast. The number of raids against fishing fleets is always a surprising feature of piracy, both in the Orient and in the West where the fishing fleets off Newfoundland were favored targets of the oceanic pirates. The "loot" was not the fish that had been caught, but the men who crewed the vessels. They were prized for their knowledge of the sea, a facet of life often seriously missing among pirate crews in later years. Pirate vessels often desperately needed pilots and seamen who knew the oceans.

Naval vessel of the early 1900s. With such ships, governments built powerful navies that finally brought an end to piracy on the oceans.

Piracy in Chinese waters lasted until recent years to a greater degree than anywhere else in the world. Piracy elsewhere was curbed by the powerful English, French and other navies which made the occupation too risky. Only another powerful government could build vessels to go against such enormous warships as Britain's *Invincible,* launched in 1907, which had a speed of over 26 knots. American and English naval vessels, and those of other western nations, were present in Chinese waters; but they were there primarily to protect their own nationals and their governments' interests in the region. So, as late as the 1920s there were well-known Chinese pirates such as Madam Hon-cho Lo, who, upon her husband's death in 1921, took command of the pirate fleet he had organized. The growth of Japanese military power and the presence of Japanese ships was important in the decline of piracy in the Orient; and the wars and naval actions of vast modern fleets, as well as the reorganization of the Chinese government, have brought piratical forays to an end in the area.

Appendixes

A. Piracy and Shipping Leagues

With such merchant groups as the Hanseatic League (originated between 1255–1262) or the Merchant Adventures (charted 1407), piracy was a two-edged sword. For instance, at its beginning the Hanseatic League united German cities because defense at sea was necessary against the swarms of pirates in the Baltic, North Sea, and elsewhere. The League successfully fought the pirates, built light houses, marked channels, fixed buoys off reefs and rocks, licensed pilots, and compiled a "sea book" as a navigational guide. All these actions helped make northern Europe, including England, commercially powerful.

Yet the ships of the Hanseatic League also engaged in piracy and destroyed competition. English traders who had formed a factory in Bergen were seized, robbed, and beaten by League members because they were exporting fish to England, a commercial activity in which the League had a monopoly. It was not uncommon for fishing boats to be attacked and sunk, and the crews killed, if they were not allied with the League. League vessels pirated both cargo and vessel of competing merchants. They raided cities, killing and burning. All the while they diligently destroyed the strongholds of other pirates throughout the North, and if they caught a competing pirate in the Baltic, such as the fierce Stortebeker, they hung him.

From the late 1500s onward the merchant warships of the Dutch and English East India Companies played a similar role. With their well-disiplined and drilled crews and their convoy system, they were usually successful in dealing with pirates at sea; but, such companies were also often responsible for acts of piracy themselves.

B. Pirate Flags

Identifying an enemy at sea has always been difficult. In ancient times sailors might have been able to recognize an enemy by the color of the vessel's sail, or by a device painted on the sail. Designs on the shields of the soldiers aboard a ship might also have been used for identifying purposes. In the mosaics in the ancient Roman port of Ostia, banners and standards can be seen on ships. Such flags have commonly been used for identification of ships.

Streamers, pennants, and flags of identity appear on both merchant and warships early in the Middle Ages. In the 1200s long, flowing streamers, or *bucans,* began to appear on ships. At sea the streamers could indicate nationality or personal identity as well as a state of hostility. By the late 1300s these streamers were sometimes longer than 30 yards, and were very wide, with complicated designs embroidered or painted on them. In 1416, for instance, the Earl of Warwick's identifying streamer showed a bear with a ragged staff, together with crosses and slashes having various meanings connected with his coat of arms. Henry the Eighth of England had the sails of one of his vessels painted gold, and had the streamers on it made of green and white, the Tudor colors, with the cross of St. George.

In the late 1600s it was common for privateers to fly their national flag, as well as a special streamer that identified them as privateers. In the 1690s a law was passed in England making the flying of such streamers manditory. Privateering streamers were hoisted for the very practical reason that, knowing the privateer's *intent,* the captain of a merchant ship could strike his own colors quickly, and thus avoid having his ship battered by cannon. Before the 1700s pirates hoisted a red flag prior to attack, to show their intent. (They were said to sail "under the Red Jack.") Sometime in the late 1600s the black pirate pennant began to appear. The Black Flag was raised after the Red Jack if the vessel the pirates intended to capture indicated resistance.

These red and black flags—sometimes they were yellow—were described simply as the Black Flag, or the Roger, or Old Roger. Roger was the slang expression for vagabond, derived from the legal term *rouge* used in the rouge laws against wandering beggers in England. Late in the 1600s, and early in the 1700s, the more flambouyant privateers and pirates began to add various symbols to their flags. Often the symbol was the skull, sometimes depicted with crossed bones, the ancient symbol of danger and death. But, skeletons, spears, hourglasses, initials, crossed cutlasses, and many other symbols were also used. One such flag depicted a skeleton with either crossed swords or bones in one hand, and in the other a glass of grog, which indicated the crew was ready for business, and primed for courage.[1] Shortly after the appearance of this device, the flag used by pirates was popularly referred to as the Jolly Roger. The use of such flags was limited, however, for the common practice of pirates of the period was to show false colors, and attack in surprise. Pirates sometimes went to great lengths to disguise their identity, sometime donning women's clothing, and prancing around deck with parasols.

---

[1]Forty bottles of rum were made ready "to fill the people with courage" aboard the ship *Nassau* in 1702, when the captain suspected attack from a suspicious ship spotted in the distance. It was the common practice at sea during these years to drink a special "leveling" amount of strong liquor before a battle. In some national navies, for example those of England and the Netherlands, such special doles of liquor were the established right of seamen and were regularly issued before combat.

C. Piracy and the Compass

Officers in charge of merchant vessels and fearful of piracy often attempted to stay clear of coasts, and this was possible once the mariner's compass came into use. No one knows with certainty when or where the mariner's compass was introduced on European vessels, nor is anyone positive about its true origin. Usually it is assumed that the magnetic compass was developed in the Orient for land use and then adopted aboard ships. It is then supposed to have entered the Mediterranean on Moslem vessels. The Egyptians, however, mentioned compass devices as early as 1650 B.C., and the ancient Greeks knew about magnetic stones and experimented with them. Compass devices have been found in the ruins of Pompey which was destroyed by a volcanic eruption in A.D. 79.

In China (Needham 1954) the magnetic compass was described in the *Ping-Chou Kho Than* in the 1100's. This stated that in dark weather a ship's pilot could "look at the south-pointing needle." Another Chinese work of that period says, "During dark or rainy days, and when nights are overclouded, sailors rely on the compass." (Centuries earlier in China magnetized floating needles had been used in geomacy, a form of divination.)

In England about 1180 Alexander Neckam, a cleric, described simple compasses in his book, *The Uses of Things,* and in France they were described about 1190 in a poem by Guiot de Provins. The best description of a primitive mariner's compass comes down to us from the writings of a French Dominican monk, Vincent de Beauvais, who early in the 1200s wrote *Speculum Majus,* the most complete scientific encyclopedia of that century. He wrote: "When the mariners are unable to find the course that should conduct them safe into port, they rub the point of a needle upon a magnet, fasten it to a straw, and place it in a vessel of water, around which they carry the magnet. The point of the needle points ever towards the magnet, and when by this means they have made the needle turn completely around, then they take away the magnet all at once. Thereupon the point of the needle turns toward the [North] star, and moves not thence." (It works, but if you attempt it don't use a metal container to hold the water!)

A fairly advanced box compass was described in 1269 by an officer in the French army, Pierre de Maricourt (Petrus Peregrimus, or Petrus Pilgrim, so called because he had been to the Holy Land on Crusade).

The year 1302 has been taken as the traditional date of the invention of the mariner's compass—that is, a compass pivoted on a needle and set on gimbals which neutralize the movement of the ship. (Gimbals are contrivances for keeping a suspended object aboard a ship horizontal.) Early in the 1300s Petrus Vesconti, perhaps the earliest of maritime cartographers, drew a coastal chart on which a pivoted needle was shown on a *rosa ventorum,* or wind rose. The claims of various writers concerning the inventor of the compass are all open to question and argument. All that can be said with any confidence is that the existence of a fairly advanced mariner's compass was known in Europe in the 1200s, and it came into wider use during the 1300s.

The design of the pivoted compass changed very little through the next five hundred years. The early compass, called a "dry compass," was found inefficient on steam vessels because the vibrations of the machinery kept it in constant motion. To overcome this, the "liquid compass" was introduced. The dry compass had already been put under a half-globe of glass, as Captain John Smith said in 1627, ". . .to keep it from dust, breaking or the wind." Now liquid, usually water and alcohol, but sometimes oil or kerosene, was put into the globe around the compass and the globe then sealed. When this was done the needle did not respond to small vibrations.

D. Women in Piracy

Aside from the Chinese woman pirate, Madame Hon-cho Lo, women seldom appeared in the history of piracy except as shore-side camp-followers. Mary Read and Anne Bonny who appeared in Johnson's *General History* (1724) are exceptions. Mary Read was born in England; Anne Bonny, in Ireland. At an early age they both commonly dressed as boys. Mary went to sea on a man-of-war at the age of thirteen. She later joined the army in Flanders, fell in love with a fellow soldier, and married. They set up an ordinary, or eating-house, but shortly afterward he died, Mary was left with debts on her hands. She then resumed her role as a man, and signed aboard a Dutch vessel sailing for the West Indies. Captured by English pirates, she stayed among them as a fellow pirate. Eventually she ended up on the ship of Captain John Rackham.

Rackham, known as *Calico Jack,* because he favored calico trousers, was accompanied by his lover, Anne Bonny. Anne, dressed as a man, fought alongside Rackham. Eventually their ship was captured. Rackham was hanged, but Anne and Mary both pleaded pregnancy (they *were* both pregnant), and their sentencing was temporarily put off. Mary Read died of a fever while awaiting the birth of her child; Anne Bonny had her child safely delivered, was reprieved, and disappeared from history.

E. Pirate Codes

The Articles of Captain Bartholomew Roberts were recorded early in the 1700s after the capture of Roberts' ship, they were taken down by the captors from one of the pirates, and are paraphrased here. The actual articles had been thrown overboard. It is suspected that they had some singularly sanguinary and gruesome clauses that were not divulged. The oath of allegiance to these articles was sworn to on a Bible. If there was any doubt whether an infringement of them had taken place, a jury was selected to pass a verdict in the matter. If an offence occurred but was not included in the articles, the offender chose a quartermaster to decide the matter. Only during battle or chase did the captain of a pirate vessel have absolute command of the men. The captain was chosen by vote, the men preferring a man who was "pistol-proof," that is not timid in battle.

ARTICLES OF BARTHOLOMEW ROBERTS

I. Every man has a vote on affairs of moment; has equal title to the fresh provisions or strong liquors at any time seized, and use of them at his pleasure unless a scarcity makes it necessary for the good of all to vote a retrenchment.

II. Every man to be called fairly in turn, by list, on board of prizes [because over and above their proper share they were on these occasions allowed a shift of clothes]. But if they defrauded the Company to the value of a dollar, in plate, jewels or money, Marooning is the punishment. If the robbery is only between one another the ears and nose of him that is guilty are to be split and he is to be set on shore, not in an unhabited place, yet somewhere where he is sure to encounter hardships.

III. No person to game at cards or dice for money.

IV. The lights and candles to be put out at eight o'clock at night. If any of the crew after that hour are still inclined to drinking, they are to do so on the open deck.

V. Pieces, pistols and cutlasses to be kept clean and fit for service.

VI. No boy or woman to be allowed. If any man is found seducing any of the latter sex, and carries her to sea disguised, he is to suffer Death.

VII. To desert the ship or quarters in battle is punishable with Death or Marooning.

VIII. No striking one another on board; every man's quarrels to be ended on shore, at sword and pistol.

IX. No man to talk of breaking up the Company till each has a share of £1,000. If, in order to do this, any man should lose a limb or become a cripple in the service, he is to have 800 dollars out of the public stock, and for lesser hurts proportionately.

X. The Captain and Quartermaster to receive two shares of a prize; the master, boatswain and gunner, one share and a half, and other officers one and a quarter.

XI. The musicians to have rest on the sabbath day, but the other six days and nights none, without special favour.

Two other sets of pirate articles are included below from between the years 1717 and 1724. They are quoted from Johnson (1829). It is easy to understand the reasoning behind some of these articles. Article VI of the *Revenge* regulations and Article IV in Roberts' list (above) clearly show how fire was so feared aboard wooden vessels, and undoubtedly many of the wooden ships reported being lost at sea went down in flames. Some of the articles Johnson himself thought would probably confuse the general reader, so he set about explaining them. In Robert's articles, Article I, concerning food and drink, he mentions that shortage of both was not an uncommon occurrence on pirate vessels. In Article II, concerning marooning, he explains that it was not necessarily an island on which a pirate was marooned, but at some desolate or uninhabited place, such as a cape. As for protecting captured women, Johnson has this comment, "So that when any fell into their hands, as it chanced in the *Onslow,* they put a sentinel immediately over her to prevent ill consequences from so dangerous an instrument of division and quarrel. But then here lies the roguery; they contend who shall be sentinal, which happens generally to be one of the greatest bullies who, to secure the lady's virtue, will let none lie with her but himself." This is a typical, almost tongue-in-cheek, Johnson remark of the sort that makes his work a pleasure to read.

ARTICLES OF CAPTAIN GEORGE LOWTHER
AND HIS COMPANY

I. The Captain is to have two full shares; the master is to have one share and a half; the doctor, mate, gunner, and boatswain, one share and a quarter.

II. He that shall be found guilty of taking up any unlawful weapon on board the privateer or any prize by us taken, so as to strike or abuse one another in any regard, shall suffer what punishment the Captain and majority of the Company shall think fit.

III. He that shall be found guilty of cowardice in the time of engagement shall suffer what punishment the Captain and Majority shall think fit.

IV. If any gold, jewels, silver etc., be found on board of any prize or prizes, to the value of a piece-of-eight, and the finder do not deliver it to the quartermaster in the space of 24 hours, [he] shall suffer what punishment the Captain and Majority shall think fit.

V. He that is found guilty of gaming, or defrauding another to the value of a shilling, shall suffer what punishment the Captain and Majority of the Company shall think fit.

VI. He that shall have the misfortune to lose a limb, in time of engagement, shall have the sum of £150 sterling, and remain with the Company as long as he shall think fit.

VII. Good quarter to be given when called for.

VIII. He that sees a sail first, shall have the best pistol or small arm on board her.

ARTICLES ON BOARD THE *REVENGE*,
JOHN PHILLIPS, CAPTAIN

I. Every man shall obey civil command; the Captain shall have one full share and a half in all prizes; the master, carpenter, boatswain and gunner shall have one share and a quarter.

II. If any man shall offer to run away or keep any secret from the company, he shall be marooned, with one bottle of Powder, one bottle of water, one small arm, and shot.

III. If any man shall steal anything in the company, or game to the value of a piece-of-eight, he shall be marooned or shot.

IV. If at any time we should meet another Marooner [that is, pirate] that man that shall sign his articles without the consent of our company shall suffer such punishment as the captain and company shall think fit.

V. That man that shall strike another whilst these articles are in force shall receive Moses's Law [that is 40 stripes lacking one] on the bare back.

VI. That man that shall snap his arms [that is pull the trigger of his gun and cause the hammer to hit the flint-lock, setting off sparks], or smoke tobacco in the hold without a cap to his pipe, or carry a candle lighted without a lanthorn [lantern], shall suffer the same punishment as the former article.

VII. That man that shall not keep his arms clean, fit for an engagement, or neglect his business, shall be cut off from his share, and suffer such other punishment as the captain and the company shall think fit.

VIII. If any man shall lose a joint in time of an engagement, he shall have 400 pieces-of-eight; if a limb, 800.

IX. If at any time you meet with a prudent woman, that man that offers to meddle with her, without her consent, shall suffer present death.

Johnson (1829) also quotes civil and statute laws concerning piracy. One states that if the master of a captured ship "gives his oath to pay a sum of money, though there be nothing taken," that is piracy. A ship at anchor, with the seamen ashore, "and a Pirate attack her and rob her, this is piracy." The last is a general law of the sea, but it did not apply in England, where such an act was considered robbery at Common Law. It was not considered piracy if necessary supplies such as food, sails, etc. were taken forcefully when they were taken "out of another ship that may spare them," and payment or promise of payment took place.

F. Early U.S. Naval Forces

The seamen in the British colonies in America had much experience at sea, not only in fishing and coastal cargo carrying, but war time experience, especially during the wars of empire (1689–1763). This war experience was mostly as privateers and not as disciplined seamen. Massachusetts alone had from 300 to 400 privateering vessels at sea from 1756 to 1763. During the seige of Boston in the autumn of 1775 George Washington organized a war time naval squadron of six schooners and a brigantine. The squadron was put together to intercept British supply ships. The first vessel commissioned was the schooner *Hannah* under Captain Nicholson Broughton. The *Hannah*, therefore, is sometimes regarded as "our first war vessel" (Westcott).

Later in the autumn of 1775 The Continental Congress appointed a "Naval Committee" to purchase and arm vessels for war. One of the first ships bought was the *Black Prince*, a three-masted merchantman that had been built in 1774. It was armed and renamed the *Alfred*, becoming the first official ship of the United Colonies Continental Navy (McCusker).

The ships of the Continental Navy mostly performed communication and convoy work, along with the capturing of British supply ships. The Continental Navy was supported by "State Navies," fitted out by all the colonies with the exception of New Jersey and Delaware. At sea the War of Independence was mostly a commercial war. During the period of hostilities the Continental Congress issued 1,697 letters of marque, and many more were issued by the states.

On March 27, 1794 the Congress of the United States passed legislation "To Provide A Naval Armament." Three frigates of 44 guns, and three of 36 guns were to be constructed. President Washington selected the names of the first three that were eventually launched in 1797: the *United States* (in May in Philadelphia), the *Constellation* (in September in Baltimore), and the *Constitution* (in October in Boston). These three frigates were the first war vessels of the United States Navy.

Bibliography

Alden, Carroll Storrs. 1936. *Lawrence Kearny: Sailor Diplomat.* Princeton: Princeton University Press.

Andrews, Kenneth R. 1967. *Drake's Voyages: A Re-Assessment of Their Place in Elizabethan Maritime Expansion.* New York: Charles Scribner's Sons.

Andrews, Kenneth R. 1964. *Elizabethan Privateering During The Spanish War 1585–1603.* Cambridge: University Press.

Armstrong, R. 1969. *The Merchantmen.* New York: Frederick A. Praegar.

Batsford, George Willes. 1922. *Hellenic History.* New York: The Macmillan Co.

Baynes, Norman H. 1925. *The Byzantine Empire.* London: Oxford University Press.

Belgrave, Charles. 1966. *The Pirate Coast (Based on the Diary of Frances Erskin Loch–Naval Commander in the Persian Gulf, 1818–1820.)* New York: Roy Publishers, Inc.

Biddulph, J. 1907. *Pirates of Malabar.* London: Smith, Elder & Co.

Bingham, W., Conroy, H., and Iklé, F. W. 1964. *A History of Asia: Formation of Civilization from Antiquity to 1600, Vol. 1.* Boston: Allyan Bacon, Inc.

Bishop, Morris. 1970. *The Middle Ages.* New York: McGraw Hill.

Bloomster, Edgar L. 1940. *Sailing and Small Craft Down The Ages.* Annapolis: U. S. Naval Institute.

Blouet, B. 1967. *A Short History of Malta.* New York: Frederick A. Praeger, Publishers.

Bradlee, F. B. C. 1923. *Piracy in the West Indies and Its Suppression.* Salem, Massachusetts: The Essex Institute.

Brand, Charles M. 1968. *Byzantium Confronts The West— 1180-1204.* Cambridge, Massachusetts: Harvard University Press.

Breasted, James Henry, 1906. *Ancient Records of Egypt: Historical Documents from The Earliest Times to The Persian Conquest, Vols. 1-5.* Reissued 1952. London: Russell & Russell, Inc.

Breasted, James Henry. 1916. *Ancient Times.* Boston: Ginn & Co.

Breasted, James Henry. 1909. *A History of Egypt.* New York: Charles Scribner's Sons.

Brown, Loyd A. 1949. *The Story of Maps.* New York: Bonanza Books.

Burney, James. 1916. *Chronological History of the Discoveries in The South Seas or Pacific Ocean, Vol. 4, West Indies: History of the Buccaneers of America.* Reprinted from the 1816 edition. London: George Allen & Unwin, Ltd.

Bury, J. B. 1912. *A History of The Eastern Roman Empire: A.D. 802-867.* Reissued 1965. London: Russell & Russell, Inc.

Carletti, Francesco. 1964. *My Voyage Around The World: 1594-1602.* Translation, H. Weinstock. New York: Pantheon Books.

Carpenter, R. 1966. *Beyond The Pillars Of Hercules.* New York: Delacorte Press.

Casson, Lionel. 1959. *The Ancient Mariners.* New York: The Macmillian Co.

Charlesworth, M. P. Second Ed. 1926. *Trade Routes and Commerce of the Roman Empire.* London: Cambridge University Press.

Childe, V. Gordon. 1953. *New Light on The Most Ancient East.* Originally published, 1928, re-written 1952. New York: Frederick A. Praeger, Publishers.

Childe, V. Gordon. 1967. *The Dawn of European Civilization.* 6th ed. New York: Alfred A. Knopf.

Cipolla, Carlo M. 1965. *Guns, Sails and Empires: Technological Innovation and The Early Phases of European Expansion, 1400-1700.* New York: Pantheon Books.

Clark, William B. 1949. *Captain Dauntless: The Story of Nicholas Biddle of The Continental Navy.* Baton Rouge: Louisiana State University Press.

Clark, William B. 1932. *Lambert Wickes, Sea Raider & Diplomat.* New Haven: Yale University Press.

Clough, S. B., Cole, C. W. 1952. *Economic History of Europe.* Boston: D. C. Heath & Co.

Course, A. G. 1966. *Pirates of The Eastern Seas.* London: Frederick Muller.

Coxere, Edward. 1946. *Adventures by Sea, 1647–1685, A Relation of Several Adventures by Sea with the Dangers, Difficulties and Hardships I Met for Several Years.* New York and London: Oxford University Press.

D'Arms, John H. 1970. *Romans on The Bay of Naples: A Social and Cultural Study of The Villas and Their Owners From 150 B.C. to A.D. 400.* Cambridge, Massachusetts: Harvard University Press.

Davies, Colin. 1970. *The Emergence of Western Society: European and English History 300–1200.* New York: Humanities Press.

Dodge, Ernest S. 1971. *Beyond The Capes: Pacific Exploration.* Boston: Little, Brown & Co.

Dow, G. F., Edmonds, J. H. 1923. *The Pirates of the New England Coast, 1630–1730.* Salem, Massachusetts: Marine Research Society.

Dowing, C. 1924. *A History of The Indian Wars With An Account of Angria The Pirate.* New York and London: Oxford University Press.

DuBoulay, F. R. H. 1970. *An Age of Ambition: English Society in the Late Middle Ages.* New York: The Viking Press.

DuChaillu, Paul B. 1898. *The Viking Age, Vol. 1.* New York: Charles Scribner's Sons.

Dudley, Donald R. 1970. *The Romans 850 B.C. – A.D. 337.* New York: Alfred A. Knopf.

Dunbabin, T. J. 1948. *The Western Greeks: A History of Sicily and South Italy from The Foundation of The Greek Colonies to 480 B.C.* Oxford: Clarendon Press.

Earle, Peter. 1970. *Corsairs of Malta and Barbary.* London: Sedgwick & Jackson.

Ehrenber, Victor. 1968. *From Solon To Socrates: Greek History and Civilization during the Sixth and Fifth Centuries B.C.* London: Methuen & Co. Ltd.

Evans, A. P., ed. 1929. *Records of Civilization—Sources and Studies.* New York: Columbia University Press.

Exquemilin, Alexandre Oliver. 1923. *The Buccaneers of America: A True Account of the Most Remarkable Assaults Committed of Late Years upon the Coasts of the West Indies.* London: George Routledge & Sons. Originally published (1678) as *De Ameri-*

canensech Zee-Rovers. Amsterdam: Jan ten Hoorn. Also published in London (1684) by Thos. Malthus, and also by W. Cooke, giving the author's name as John Esqumelin and the title as *The Bucaners of America.*

Fairbanks, John K., Reischauer, Edwin O., Craig, Albert M. 1960. *East Asia: The Modern Transformation.* Boston: Houghton Mifflin Co.

Fairbanks, J. K. 1953. *Trade and Diplomacy on the Chinese Coast.* Cambridge, Massachusetts: Harvard University Press.

Fowler, E. W. 1965. *English Sea Power in the Early Tudor Period, 1485–1558.* Ithica: Cornell University Press.

Fox, Grace. 1940. *British Admirals and Chinese Pirates.* London: Rutledge & Kegan Paul.

French, Joseph Lewis, ed. 1922. *Great Pirate Stories,* 2 vols. (R. Glasspoole, "The Terrible Landrones"; Stanley Lane-Poole, "Galleys and Galley Slaves"; H. C. St. John, "The Wild Coast of Nippon." Originally published (1922) by Brentano's. Reprinted, 1937. New York: Tudor Publishing Co.

Gibbon, Edward. 1946. *The History of the Decline and Fall of the Roman Empire.* New York: Limited Edition Club.

Glover, Terrot Reaveley. 1901. *Life and Letters in the Fourth Century.* London: Russell & Russell. Reissued 1968.

Goitein, S. D. 1967. *A Mediterranean Society: Economic Foundations, The Mediterranean in The Eleventh Century.* Berkeley and Los Angeles: University of California Press.

Goldolphin, F., ed. 1942. *The Greek Historians.* New York: Random House.

Grey, C. 1933. *Pirates of the Eastern Seas, 1618–1723.* London: Sampson, Low, Marston & Co.

Guttridge, L. F. and Smith, J. D. 1969. *The U. S. Navy in the Age of Sail.* New York: Harper & Row.

Harden, Donald. 1963. *The Phoenicians.* Vol. 26 of *Ancient People,* G. Daniel, Gen. Ed. New York: Frederick A. Praeger.

Hargreaves, Reginald. 1959. *The Narrow Seas: A History of The English Channel.* London: Sedgwick & Jackson, Ltd.

Haring, C. H. 1910. *The Buccaneers in the West Indies in XVII Century.* London: Methuen & Co. Ltd.

Harris, Arthur M. 1923. *Pirate Tales From The Law.* Boston: Little, Brown, & Co.

Herodotus. 1954. *The Histories.* Translated by A. de Sélincourt. Baltimore: Penguin Books.

Holmes, George. 1962. *The Later Middle Ages, 1271-1485*. Edinburgh: Nelson.

Holmes, U. T. 1952. *Daily Living in the 12th Century, based on the Observations of Alexander Necham*. Madison: University of Wisconsin Press.

Homer. 1959. *The Odyssey*. Translation by S. H. Butcher and Andrew Lang. New York: Dodd, Mead & Co.

Hornell, James. 1941. Sea-Trade in Early Times. *Antiquity*.

Hourani, George Fadlo. 1951. *Arab Seafaring in The Indian Ocean in Ancient and Early Medieval Times*. Princeton: Princeton University Press.

Hughson, Shirley C. 1894. *The Carolina Pirates and Colonial Commerce*. Baltimore: Johns Hopkins University Press.

Hussey, J. M. Editor. 1966. *The Cambridge Medieval History*, Vol. IV: *The Byzantine Empire*. London and New York: Cambridge University Press.

Jackson, Melvin H. 1969. *Privateers in Charleston, 1793-1796*. Washington: Smithsonian Institution Press.

Jameson, John Franklin. 1923. *Privateering and Piracy in the Colonial Period*. New York: The Macmillan Co.

Johnson, Charles. 1829. *A General History of the Robberies and Murders of the Most Notorious Pyrates, and also their Policies, Discipline and Government, from their first Rise and Settlement in the Island of Providence, in 1717, to the present year 1724*. American publication, Henry Benton, Hartford, Connecticut.

Karraker, Cyrus H. 1953. *Piracy, Was A Business*. Rindge, New Hampshire: Richard R. Smith Publishing Co., Inc.

Kramer, Samuel N. 1959. *History Begins at Sumer*. New York: Doubleday & Co.

Landstrom, Bjorn. 1961. *The Ship—An Illustrated History*. New York: Doubleday & Co., Inc.

Lane, Frederic C. 1966. *Venice and History: The collected papers of Frederic C. Lane*. Baltimore: Johns Hopkins Press.

Lane, Frederic C. 1973. *Venice, A Maritime Republic*. Baltimore: The Johns Hopkins Press.

Levick, Barbara. 1967. *Roman Colonies*. Oxford: Clarendon Press.

Lewis, Archibald R. 1951. *Naval Power and Trade in the Mediterranean A.D. 500-1100*. Princeton: Princeton University Press.

Lewis, N. and Reinhold, M., eds. 1951. *Roman Civilization: Selected Readings, Vol. 1, The Republic*. New York: Columbia University Press.

Lewis, W. H. 1957. *The Splendid Century: Life in the France of Louis XIV.* New York: Doubleday & Co.

Lindsay, Jack. 1968. *The Ancient World: Manners & Morals.* New York: G. P. Putnam's Son.

Lloyd, Alan. 1968. *The Spanish Centuries.* New York: Doubleday & Co, Inc.

Lloyd, Christopher. 1966. *William Dampier. (The Sweet trade of privateering in the 1600s.)* London: Faber & Faber.

Lucas, F. L. 1951. *Greek Poetry.* New York: The Macmillian Co.

Mahan, A. T. 1894. *The Influence of Sea Power upon the French Revolution and Empire, 1793-1812.* Vol. 1. Boston: Little, Brown, and Company.

Marcus, G. J. 1961. *A Naval History of England: The Formative Centuries.* Boston: Little, Brown & Co.

McCusker, John J. 1973. *Alfred, The First Continental Flagship.* Washington: Smithsonian Institution Press.

Meiggs, Russel. 1960. *Roman Ostia.* Oxford: Clarendon Press.

Miles, S. B. 1919. *The Countries & Tribes of The Persian Gulf.* London: Harrison & Sons.

Miller, William. 1908. *The Latins in the Levant: A History of Frankish Greece 1204-1566.* Reprinted New York: Barnes & Noble, Inc., 1964.

Mireaux, Emile. 1959. *Daily Life in The Time of Homer.* (Originally published, Librarie Hachette, 1959.) Translated by I. Sells. London: George Allen & Unwin, Ltd.

Mommsen, Theodor. 1887. *The Provinces of The Roman Empire.* Translation by W. P. Dickson. Chicago: The University of Chicago Press, 1968.

Mommsen, Theodor. *The History of Rome.* 1959. C. Bryans and F. J. R. Hendy, eds. New York: Philosophical Library, Inc.

Moore, R. W. 1942. *The Roman Commonwealth.* London: The English University Press.

Morris, Charles. 1898. *Historical Tales of Japan & China.* Philadelphia: J. P. Lippincott Co.

Myres, John L. 1953. *Geographical History in Greek Islands.* Oxford: Clarendon Press.

Neale, J. E. 1934. *Queen Elizabeth I.* London: Jonathan Cape.

Needham, Joseph. 1954. *Science and Civilization in China, Vol. 4, Nautics.* Cambridge; The University Press.

Norman, C. B. 1887. *The Corsairs of France.* London: Low, Marston, Searle, and Rivington.

O'Dell, A. C. 1957. *The Scandinavian World: Geographies for Advanced Study.* S. H. Beaver, ed. London: Longman's, Green & Co.

Ormerod, Henry A. 1924. *Piracy in The Ancient World: An Essay in Mediterranean History.* Liverpool: The University Press of Liverpool.

Parker, H. M. D. 1958. *A History of the Roman World A.D. 138–337.* Revised from the 1935 edition by B. H. Warmington. London: Methuen & Co., Ltd.

Pendle, George. 1963. *A History of Latin America.* Baltimore: Penguin Books.

Ploetz, Carl. 1883. *Epitome of History.* Translated and enlarged W. H. Tillinghast. New York: Blue Ribbon Books, 1914.

Polo, Marco. n. d. *The Travels.* New York: The Orion Press Edition.

Potter, E. B., ed. 1955. *The United States and World Sea Power.* Englewood Cliffs, N. J.: Prentice Hall.

Prichard, J. B. 1955. *Ancient Near East Texts.* 2nd ed. Princeton: Princeton University Press.

Rankin, H. F. 1969. *The Golden Age of Piracy.* Williamsburg, Virginia: Colonial Williamsburg Inc.

Reischauer, Edwin O., Fairbanks, John K. 1958. *East Asia: The Great Tradition.* Boston: Houghton Mifflin Co.

Robinson, C. E. 1933. *Everyday Life in Ancient Greece.* Oxford: Clarendon Press.

Rostovtzeff, M. 1957. *The Social and Economic History of the Roman Empire, Revised by P. M. Frazer.* Oxford: Clarendon Press.

Salmon, Edward T. 1944. *A History of The Roman World from 30 B.C. to A.D. 138.* New York: The Macmillian Co.

Savelle, Max, ed. 1957. *A History of World Civilization,* Vol. 1. New York: Henry Holt & Co.

Schliemann, Heinrich. 1884. *Troja: Results of the Latest Researches and Discoveries on the Site of Homer's Troy.* 1967 edition. Benjamin Blom.

Schurz, William Lytle. 1939. *The Manila Galleon.* New York: E. P. Dutton.

Scullard, Howard H. 1967. *The Etruscan Cities and Rome.* Ithaca: Cornell University Press.

Scullard, Howard. H. 1959. *From the Gracchi to Nero: A History of Rome from 133 B.C. to A.D. 68.* London: Methuen & Co., Ltd.

Scullard, Howard H. 1951. *A History of the Roman World from 753 to 146 B.C.* London: Methuen & Co., Ltd.

Sherk, Robert K. 1969. *Roman Documents from The Greek East.* Baltimore: Johns Hopkins Press.

Smith, John. 1627. *A Sea Grammer with the Plaine Exposition of Smith's Accidence for Young Seamen, Enlarged.* 1970 edition. London: Micheal Joseph Ltd.

Starr, Chester G. 1962. *The Origins of Greek Civilization 1100–650 B.C.* London: Jonathan Cape.

Starr, Chester G. 1941. *The Roman Imperial Navy.* 2nd ed. 1960. New York: Barnes & Noble, Inc.

Statarn, E. P. 1910. *Privateers and Privateering.* London: Hutchinson & Co.

Sternbeck, Alfred. 1942. *Filibusters & Buccaneers.* New York: National Travel Club.

Tacitus. 1948. *The Agricola and the Germania.* Translated by H. Mattingly, 1929. Baltimore: Penquin Books.

Taylour, William. 1964. *The Mycenaeans.* New York: Frederick A. Praeger.

Thompson, James Westfall. 1928. *Economic and Social History of The Middle Ages, 300–1300.* 2 vol. 1959 ed. New York: Frederick Ungar Pub. Co.

Thompson, James Westfall. 1931. *Economic and Social History of Europe in the Late Middle Ages, 1300–1500.* 1960 ed. New York: Frederic Ungar Pub. Co.

Thorndike, Lynn. 1917. *The History of Medieval Europe.* 1949 ed. Boston: Houghton Mifflin Co.

Thucydides. *The Histories.* Translated by B. Jowett. Oxford: The Clarendon Press, 1900.

Torr, Cecil. *Ancient Ships, with an Appendix Containing a Series of Articles on Greek Warships and the Greek Trireme by W. W. Tarn, A. B. Cook, W. Richardson, P. H. Newman, and C. Torr.* 1964 ed. Chicago: Argonaut Inc., Publishers.

Toynbee, Arnold J. 1959. *Hellenism: The History of Civilization.* New York and London: Oxford University Press.

Trevelyn, G. M. 1944. *English Social History: A Survey of Six Centuries, Chaucer to Queen Victoria.* London: Longmans.

Trevlyan, G. M. 1926. *History of England.* Vol. II. *The Tudor and Stuart Era.* Reprinted 1953. New York: Doubleday & Co.

Tunstall, Brian. 1936. *The Realities of Naval History.* London: George Allen & Unwin Ltd.

Ullmann, Walter. 1966. *The Individual & Society in the Middle Ages.* Baltimore: Johns Hopkins Press.

Ure, P. N. 1922. *The Origin of Tyranny.* New York: Russell & Russell.

Vacano, Otto William. 1960. *The Etruscans in the Ancient World.* Translated by S. A. Ogilvie. New York: St. Martin's Press.

Verrill, A. Hyatt. 1923. *The Real Story of the Pirate (West Indies).* New York & London: D. Appleton & Co.

Walbank, F. W. 1969. *The Awful Revolution: The Decline of the Roman Empire in the West.* Toronto: University of Toronto Press.

Ward, Ralph T. 1973. *Ships Throrgh History.* Indianapolis and New York: The Bobbs-Merrill Company, Inc.

Ward, Ralph T. 1973. *Steamboats: A History of the Early Adventure.* Indianapolis and New York: The Bobbs-Merrill Company, Inc.

Westcott, Allan, ed. 1947. *American Sea Power Since 1775.* Philadelphia, Chicago, New York: J. B. Lippincott Co.

Whatmough, Joshua. 1937. *The Foundation of Roman Italy.* London: Methuen & Co. Ltd.

Wilkin, Robert N. 1947. *Eternal Lawyer: A Legal Biography of Cicero.* New York: The Macmillan Co.

Wilson, David M. 1970. *The Vikings and their Origins: Scandinavia in the First Milennium.* London: Thames & Hudson.

Winston, Alexander. 1969. *No Man Knows My Grave: Privateers and Pirates, 1665–1715.* Boston: Houghton Mifflin Co.

Woodroofe, T. 1958. *Vantage at Sea: England's Emergence as an Oceanic Power.* New York: St. Martin's Press.

Young, E., Helweg-Larsen, K. 1965. *The Pirate Priest: The Life of Père Labat in the West Indies, 1693–1705.* London: Jarrolds.

Zinmern, Alfred. 1931. *The Greek Commonwealth: Politics and Economics in Fifth-Century Athens.* Oxford: Clarendon Press.

Index

Designed by EditaGraphics, Annapolis, Md.

Composed in Aldine with Codex display
by Jones Composition Company.

Printed on 60 lb. WW&F Mystery Opaque White
by Collins Lithographing and Printing Company.

Bound in Roxite C #57549
by Complete Books Company.